ELTHAM
IN THE

VOLUME ONE

From Roman Times until 1939

© THE ELTHAM SOCIETY

ISBN 0-9515907-0-7

Published by the Eltham Society
c/o "South Ende Greene",
　　1, Clare Corner,
　　New Eltham,
　　London SE9 2AE

Editor Roger Simmons. F.I.S.T.C.

Typeset in 12pt Courier Font on A4 by Sally Simmons.

Illustrations by Philip Johnston and Jason Smith.

Cover and prelims designed by Sian Rogers.

Maps of 1605 and 1839 drawn by Jason Smith.

Photographs obtained from the following collections:

B.F.C.	*Bert French Collection.*
E.S.C.	*Eltham Society Collection.*
G.W.C.	*Gus White Collection.*
J.K.C.	*John Kennett Collection.*
S.F.C.	*Simmons Family Collection.*

THE ELTHAM SOCIETY
Founded in 1965

Preserving the Past
Conserving the Present
Protecting the Future

ELTHAM IN THE MAKING

CONTENTS

ACKNOWLEDGEMENTS

The Eltham Society acknowledges with gratitude the many individuals who have so generously contributed to the publication of "Eltham In The Making".

Particularly, we thank Margaret Evans for her assistance with detail on the Shaw family, 18th century and early 20th century Eltham. We also thank John Priestley for allowing us to use his transcripts of manorial documents and providing information on medieval Eltham.

We are also grateful to Julian Watson, Local History Librarian for the London Borough of Greenwich, and his staff at "Woodlands", Mycenae Road, Blackheath, for their help and encouragement. The Eltham Society's archives are deposited at "Woodlands" and have been extensively used in the research for this book.

Especially, we thank Honorary Member Mrs Gladys Perkins for a donation made in memory of her sister, Miss "Cissie" Langton, and other Members of the Society who have given donations and subscriptions. Without their generosity, publication would not have been possible.

Thanks are also due to the following organisations who have provided sponsorship and advertisments:

> **Barclays Bank plc**
> **Kent Archaeological Society**
> **Marc Fitch Fund**
> **National Westminster Bank plc**
> **Bernard H. Skinner & Co.**
> **Woolwich Equitable Building Society**

"Eltham In The Making" is published in association with the London Borough of Greenwich.

CHAIRMAN'S FOREWORD

The residents of Eltham are fortunate to live in a pleasant London suburb, and one which has a very interesting and well recorded history.

It is over eighty years since R.R.C. Gregory's "The Story of Royal Eltham" was published. Unfortunately, this history of our area is now most difficult to obtain. It was compiled as separate articles rather than a chronological history. Change has been so rapid in our century that many a present day resident fails to recognise the sites and locations which were landmarks to this Edwardian author.

The Council of the Eltham Society therefore agreed that a new, chronologically arranged, yet concise account of Eltham's history should be written as part of the Society's twenty fifth anniversary celebrations. Many years of work and research by members of the Society have produced a book which will be an invaluable source of reference to be enjoyed by present and future generations of "Elthamians" everywhere.

The authors and the editor have contrived succinctly to tell the story of the ordinary residents' daily lives. They have effectively linked the past centuries to our surroundings in the 1990's. We hope it will prove an inspiration for further research into Eltham's history, an encouragement to the conservation of what is best in our present suburb and possibly even a guide towards improving the quality of life for future residents. Eventually, we hope there will be a sequel volume continuing the story from 1939 to date.

Meanwhile, I commend "Eltham In The Making" to all who seek a knowledge of Eltham and an understanding of its history, or simply, a good read.

Clifford Crate

Clifford Crate,
Chairman, The Eltham Society, 1990.

THE ELTHAM SOCIETY

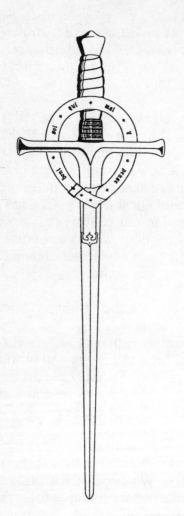

Our Aims and Objectives

Preserving the Past

To stimulate public interest in and care for the beauty, history and character of the Town and its surroundings

Conserving the Present

To encourage the preservation and improvement of features of general public amenity and interest by fighting against what is unsightly and despoiled, and fighting for environmentally acceptable standards throughout Eltham.

Protecting the Future

To encourage high standards in the architecture and planning of building developments, by the constant vetting of planning applications and also the maintenance of listed and historical buildings.

To pursue these ends the Society publishes a quarterly Newsletter which often contains articles of a local history nature. Meetings are held at Eltham Hill School on the 1st Thursday of each month apart from the months of January, April, August and September.

For membership information please contact The Membership Secretary, whose address can be obtained from Eltham Library.

IN THE BEGINNING

It may never be known when Eltham was first inhabited but it is evident that the natural resources of the area could have supported human life from earliest times. Streams and ponds provided ample water and woodland supplied timber for fuel and shelter. Abundant animals and plants provided food for these earliest of residents. With the development of agriculture the lighter soils in the present High Street area would have been most suitable for early ploughs. The meadows alongside the Quaggy and Wyncham Streams provided grass for the grazing of animals. Neolithic flint artefacts have been found in Mottingham, Welling, East Wickham and Blackheath. Bronze Age artefacts have been found in Woolwich, Erith and Bexleyheath. As yet, nothing of these early periods has been found in Eltham but there is plenty of evidence for human existence in the surrounding districts and Eltham's amenities were at least their equal.

Only after the Roman invasion in 43 A.D. is there any evidence of settlement in Eltham. However, it would be most unwise to assume that this was the first settlement within the district now called Eltham. Modern research in landscape-history seems to indicate that most of England was cultivated several centuries before the Roman conquest. A farmstead dating from the 1st century A.D. was found during the building of the War Memorial Hospital on Shooters Hill and another was discovered during house construction in Archery Road. A Roman building, possibly a bath house, was found in Mottingham in 1939 whilst an air raid shelter was being constructed. Two Roman cremation urns, dating from c.160 A.D. were found in Glenesk Road. Other Roman sites are known in Charlton, Greenwich, Woolwich, Plumstead and along the valley of the River Cray.

Glenesk Road Roman Pots

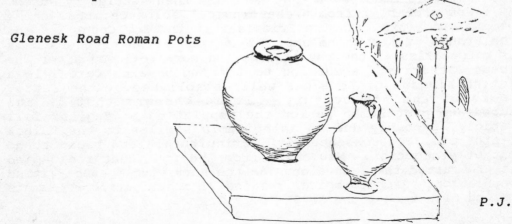

P.J.

The Roman Watling Street, which crossed Shooters Hill, is mentioned in the Antonine Itinerary which, dating from c.200 A.D., describes the major highways, not only in Britain but throughout the Roman Empire. The modern road over Shooters Hill, the A207, lies almost on the same alignment as the Roman road. The slight deviation from the original alignment is seen most clearly at night, by observing the street lights from the top of the hill.

A207 Shooters Hill looking west from Welling,
1989
                                                        S.F.C.

At the beginning of the 5th century the last Roman legions were withdrawn from Britain. The 8th century writer, the Venerable Bede, says that Kent was then settled by Jutes. It seems probable, from archaeological evidence, that these people had links with the Friesians in the Low Countries and the Franks of the Rhineland. The first Jutish settlers came as mercenaries in the pay of Rome and more followed after the Roman withdrawal. According to the Anglo-Saxon Chronicle a Jutish Kingdom of Kent was well established by the latter years of the 5th century. It is thought that in the immediate post Roman period the population of England fell rapidly, probably due to an epidemic similar to the "Black Death" of 1349. Consequently, agricultural land began to go out of production. Newcomers from the Continent reoccupied it and farmed the land alongside the surviving Romano-British population. Archaeological remains of a hut dating from this period have been found at St. Mary Cray.

The district we know as Eltham became part of the Jutish Kingdom of Kent. This kingdom was divided into lathes or provinces for judicial and taxation purposes. Each lathe was centred on a royal estate and had a region of good arable soils bordering the River Thames or its estuary and an area of woodland in the Weald. Eltham was in the Lathe of Sutton (Sutton at Hone). The royal estate was centred upon Dartford and the Lathe stretched from the Thames-side between Deptford and Dartford to the Sussex border near Edenbridge. Later, the lathes were subdivided into "hundreds." Eltham was situated within the Hundred of Greenwich, later called Blackheath Hundred.

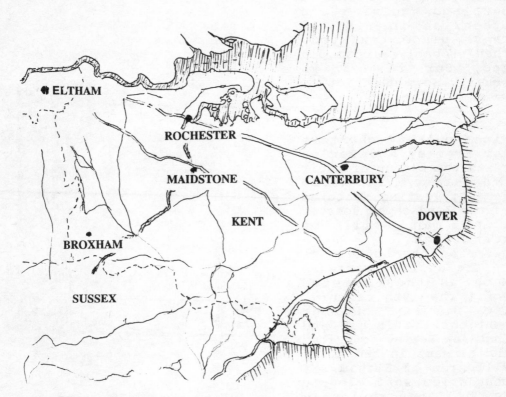

Map of Kent showing relationship between Eltham and its "den"   P.J.

The Wealden woods were important for the people of Kent for it was here that the herds of pigs were driven in autumn to fatten on the acorns and beech mast before the winter slaughter. Each community had its own part of the woods called a "den." (The dens for the Lathe of Sutton were near Edenbridge and Cowden.) Eltham's dens have been identified as being around Broxham, near Edenbridge.

As yet no evidence of Saxon/Jutish Eltham has come to light. However, present historical thought suggests that villages, as we know them, did not then exist. Settlement was in the form of single or groups of two or three farmsteads. This may well have been the case for Eltham. As Eltham is not mentioned by name until the Domesday Book of 1086 we must look elsewhere for clues to its existence.

Many of our neighbouring communities are known to have existed before 1086 as they are mentioned in Anglo Saxon charters. Erith appears in 695, Bexley in 765, Lewisham, Bromley and Mottingham in 862, and Woolwich and Greenwich in 918. If these places existed, then probably Eltham did too, for it was an equally good district in which to live.

Ninth century charters for Bromley and Bexley trace the extent of their boundaries in some detail, listing features of the landscape, some of which can still be identified. Both describe the boundaries of the ancient parishes much as they existed until the 19th century. The Bromley charter mentions Mottingham and that for Bexley describes the streams in the Avery Hill area of Eltham. If boundaries were clearly defined then obviously some place was on the other side - Eltham and Mottingham.

Borough Boundary Stone on River Shuttle at Avery Hill   *J.S.*

It has already been said that boundaries were defined by the ninth century, usually by describing recognisable features of the landscape. A study of Eltham's boundary as defined in a survey of Eltham in 1605 (now in the Public Record Office) together with later maps, shows that much of it follows features of the landscape. Across Shooters Hill the boundary follows the line of Roman Watling Street. Towards Lee, the Lower Kid Brook and the River Quaggy form a natural border between Eltham and Kidbrooke. A tributary of the Quaggy forms a boundary between Eltham and Mottingham, as does Mottingham Road. Parts of the eastern boundary follow now culverted streams, tributaries of the River Shuttle, shown on 19th century Ordnance Survey maps. It is therefore probable that these are the ancient boundaries of Eltham dating back at least to the 9th century. Some of these boundaries still survive to the present day, dividing the London Borough of Greenwich from its neighbouring boroughs of Bexley and Bromley.

Boundary Mark at Shooters Hill showing the junction of the parishes of Eltham, Kidbrooke and Charlton, 1989   *S.F.C.*

Another reminder of these ancient times is to be found in our road pattern. Apart from 20th century by-passes and the mass of residential streets, our road system developed in an early period to provide links with neighbouring communities. Such ancient links include the roads to Bexley, Footscray, Lee and Chislehurst. Well Hall Road follows the course of the old highway to Woolwich except for the portion between the High Street and the railway bridge which dates only from 1905. Other old roads still exist as footpaths, like Gravel Pit Lane, Stoney Alley and Butterfly Lane.

Although we have no documentary source for Eltham's existence until 1086 there is sufficient evidence to show that it was then an old settlement.

Man has lived in Eltham for at least 2000 years but its origins are lost in the mists of time.

Gravel Pit Lane, Bexley Road, 1989   *S.F.C.*

ROYALTY AND PEASANTS

In 1086 the Domesday Book was compiled and within its pages is the first documentary evidence for Eltham's existence. (In translation)

"Hamo the Sheriff holds Eltham from the Bishop. It answers for 1½ sulongs. Land for 12 ploughs. 42 villagers with 12 small holders have 11 ploughs. 9 slaves. Meadow 22 acres. woodland 50 pigs. Value before 1066 £16, when acquired £12, now £20. Alfwold held it from the King."

The Domesday Book refers to the estate of Eltham, from Shooters Hill in the north, to Chislehurst in the south, Blackfen in the east and to Lee in the west, not just the High Street area. The name "Eltham" is usually taken to mean "Elta's Homestead" and is probably of Anglo-Saxon origin. The Bishop was Odo, Bishop of Bayeux, a half brother of William the Conqueror. Hamo, who originated from Evreux in northern France, was a distant relative of William. Alfwold (or Aethelwold as it is spelt in another entry in the Domesday Book) had the right to hold a court in Eltham and owned the estate. It is not known whether he was a resident landlord or had other estates. Other Aethelwolds are mentioned in the Kent Domesday, some still holding land in 1086, but none can be identified as Aethelwold of Eltham.

The sulong is a term found only in Kent as a measure of arable land and scholars have long debated its meaning. It is probably some form of tax assessment on land under the plough. The plough lands, estimated at about 1800 acres, would be found on the higher, well drained parts of Eltham and the meadow lay near the River Quaggy and Wyncham Stream.

P.J.

A Kentish Plough

13

In Kent, woodland was not assessed in acres but in the number of pigs that were paid as rent to the lord of the manor in return for the use of the woods. The usual rent was one pig for every seven a man possessed. Eltham probably had in the region of 350 pigs which grazed in the woods in autumn to fatten on the acorns. These woods still exist on Shooters Hill where botanical evidence indicates that these are ancient woodlands, which have never been cultivated. The soil is poor and unsuitable for cultivation but these woods provided a crop in the form of timber for building and wood for fences, tools and firewood.

Shooters Hill Woods in winter, c. 1983   *S.F.C.*

From the number of inhabitants listed it can be estimated that the total population was about 270. Apart from a small amount of 11th century pottery found at Eltham Palace we have no evidence as to where they lived but the ancient hamlets of Well Hall, Southend and Pope Street (New Eltham) may be the original farmsteads of Eltham. Other dwellings may have been in the vicinity of the church.

Eltham was a valuable estate, richer than its neighbours Charlton, Lee, Greenwich, Plumstead and Wricklemarsh. Lewisham, with its market, port and mills was a more valuable estate, as was Bexley on the River Cray with its mills. It is possible that Woolwich is included in the Eltham entry. The Domesday entry for Woolwich is only 63 acres and is thought by some local historians to refer to North Woolwich across the Thames. Mottingham is included in Lewisham's entry as both belonged to the Abbey Of Ghent.

No church is mentioned for Eltham. Churches are mentioned for some places, usually holdings of the Archbishop of Canterbury. It may be that the Domesday Commissioners used existing manorial records which listed churches to compile those entries. However, it must not be assumed that these were the only churches in Kent. Many Kentish churches have evidence of pre-conquest foundation and the county had been Christian for almost 400 years. Village or estate churches were established well before the 11th century. No date can be given for the foundation of the church in Eltham. The present parish church of St. John the Baptist is Victorian but its predecessor stood on almost the same site, certainly from the beginning of the 12th century and probably much longer. The "Textus Roffensis" is a document of c.1115, in the possession of Rochester Cathedral. It lists many of the churches in the Diocese of Rochester, to which Eltham then belonged, and mentions Eltham. Photographs taken in the 19th century of the previous church seem to indicate a building dating in part from this period. The first known priest was Adam de Bromleigh in 1160. In the construction of the present church a carved stone coffin was found, again of 12th century origin.

The old Parish Church of St. John the Baptist before rebuilding in 1875

E.S.C.

On Hamo's death his lands were inherited by his niece, Mathilda, who was married to an illegitimate son of Henry I, Robert, Earl of Gloucester. Eltham thus became part of the Earldom of Gloucester. These estates, including Eltham, passed, by marriage, to the De Clare family of Tonbridge, Kent, who then took the title, Earl of Gloucester. In 1166 the then Earl of Gloucester presented Eltham Church to Keynsham Abbey near Bristol, with whom it remained until the dissolution of the monasteries in the reign of Henry VIII.

By 1263, when a survey was carried out, the manor of Eltham had been sub-divided into two parts, one portion was held by the Gloucester family and the other by the Mandevilles. When this sub-division of the Domesday Manor occurred is not known. Gilbert de Clare, 8th Earl of Gloucester, granted his part of Eltham to John de Vesci who held land mainly in the North, including Alnwick Castle. This is recalled in the name Alnwick Road at Horn Park. De Vesci settled Eltham upon his illegitimate son, William, and appointed Anthony Bek, Bishop of Durham to hold the estate in trust until the boy came of age. Bishop Bek occupied the estate and began building himself a residence where Eltham Palace now stands. The moat and the lower portions of the moat walls from his manor house survive and can still be seen. Excavations in 1975-1979 revealed the lower courses of his great hall with a fine tiled floor still in situ. William de Vesci seems never to have been in possession of Eltham, for, in 1305, the Bishop ceded the estate to the Crown. The Mandeville holdings do not seem to become part of the Crown estates until later in the 14th century and it is uncertain whether all their land passed into royal possession. The land ownership of Eltham for the early Middle Ages is unclear as many documents, over the centuries, have been lost.

Moat Bridge at Eltham Palace, 1989   *J.K.C.*

A market charter was granted to Eltham in 1285 allowing a weekly market and a yearly fair to be held on the eve of the Feast of the Holy Trinity and lasting three days. The charter was renewed in 1439. The market, according to Hasted in his "Topography and History of Kent" which was published in 1797, had long since been discontinued. The renewed charter allowed four annual fairs, all for the sale of cattle and horses, on Palm Sunday, Easter Monday, Whitsun Monday and October 10th, the feast of St. Paulinus of Rochester. Again, Hasted says these survived until the beginning of the 18th century. Evidence for the market and fairs is very scanty. It could be that Eltham's market was one of the many throughout England that did not flourish.

Tudor Barn and Moat, Well Hall, 1989   *S.F.C.*

During the 13th century the trees alongside Watling Street over Shooters Hill were cleared, by order of Edward I, to prevent attacks on travellers by highway robbers. Documents of this century refer to Shooters Hill as "Shitereshelle," possibly meaning "the hill of the small streams." Many small streams are found on Shooters Hill. The moat at Well Hall also dates from this century. Such moats surrounding small manor houses, as was Well Hall, were fashionable at this period and a status symbol for the owner rather than a defensive construction. The first documented owner of Well Hall is Matthew de Hegham in 1253, but the site is probably of earlier origin.

The 14th and 15th centuries saw many visits to Eltham by the monarch and his court. The creation of a royal residence made a considerable impact upon the lives of the residents of Eltham. In the early 14th century farmland was enclosed to form the Royal Deer Parks. The Great Park was enclosed around 1315. Middle Park may also have been enclosed at about the same time but, curiously, in some documents it is also called the "Old Park," so it could be even older. Horn Park was enclosed later, in 1465. Surviving documents show that small pieces of land were added to the parks over the next three centuries. Deer were important to the medieval economy both for sport and ensuring a winter supply of fresh meat for the royal table. Most cattle were slaughtered in the autumn and the meat salted to preserve it. Fresh venison was a valuable commodity for the Crown as well as a welcome luxury.

The periodic visits of the Court did not interrupt the farming year of the residents of Eltham, although good farmland had become deer park. Many lived in the High Street area where the medieval layout has partially survived to the present century. Some of the High Street property boundaries have remained almost unchanged since they were laid out in the 12th or 13th centuries, perhaps when the deer parks were enclosed. Only the buildings have changed. The rear gardens and yards stretch back to the old back lanes now known as Philipot Path and Orangery Lane.

Philipot Path on southern side of the
High Street, 1990   S.F.C.

An insight into life for Eltham inhabitants can be gained from surviving manorial documents for Eltham Mandeville for the years 1318-1325. This was a period of turbulence in England with rebellion against Edward II, inspired by his Queen, Isabella, a frequent visitor to Eltham. Their second son, John of Eltham, was born at Eltham Palace in the summer of 1316.

Eltham Mandeville appears to have been a scattered holding in Eltham but it also possessed parts of Mottingham, Woolwich and an area called "Wiklond" which may be North Woolwich. In the year 1322 to 1323 Hugh de Lee was the "Steward and Receiver" of the Manor of Mandeville and Mitcham for the Lord of the Manor, Geoffery le Scrop who held it from the Mandeville family.

Rent from Eltham Mandeville and Mottingham for the terms of Christmas, Easter, the Nativity of John the Baptist and Michaelmas were, in total, 50s 3d. Two cocks and 13 hens brought in 2s 5d rent at Christmas together with 110 eggs at Easter worth 5½d. Wiklond returned a rent of 73 shillings 3 farthings for the same terms. Seven cocks and 28 hens gave a rent of 5s 6½d at Christmas and 242 eggs were worth 12d at Easter. The pannage of pigs in the Mandeville woods raised 51s 10d. In all £14 3s 4½d was received. However, £8 15s 9d was paid out in rent to the Lord of the Manor of Eltham (the King) for land in Eltham. This included 1 pound weight of pepper. John de Henley also received 9 shillings in rent for his tenements.

Thomas Dun was the Sergeant of Mandeville, responsible for the day to day running of the estate. His accounts show the income and expenditure of the manor. The sale of corn brought in 108s 11d. This included the sale of wheat, maslin (a mixture of wheat and rye), dredge (a mix of barley and oats for horses) and beans. Livestock included cows, pigs, piglets, poultry and eggs were sold for £4 7s 9d. Milk from 6 cows was sold for 36 shillings. The old apple orchard was cut down and 24 shillings was received for the wood. A new apple orchard was planted in that year in the garden of Mandeville at a cost of 18s 2½d. Hugh le Cavel was paid 2s 6d for 12 days working to make the new orchard. Five men were also hired for six days at a total cost of 5 shillings to assist him. Apple trees were bought at 1½d or 2d each from several people including Gilbert le Medior, Maud Ingol of Lewisham, Walter the Miller, Edward ate Broke and Anys King of Mottingham. In all, 75 young apple trees were purchased and planted.

Crops grown were wheat, barley, oats, rye, peas, beans and vetch. From the woodland, bavins (small faggots) were made for firewood. Farm animals included cart-horses, stots (ponies), cows, oxen for pulling the ploughs, pigs and chickens. Excess produce was sold, probably in London, and some was sent to Geoffery le Scrop's house in the capital. Expenditure on ploughs was very high - 20s 4½d, most of it going on repairing the iron plough-shares. Medieval iron was very brittle, so it broke easily on stoney soil. Maintenance of the grange or manor house cost 7s 7d. The grange was re-roofed and a new window made. A carpenter repaired the chapel and made a "byre" under it to house the calves. These early records indicate a sizeable grange but its location is unknown. Drainage of the fields was important and 6s was spent on clearing out old ditches and making new ones. Several fields are mentioned by name but only one can be located with some certainty. This is "Nelesfeld" which, with the aid of the 1605 Survey of the Manor of Eltham, can be located along the Bexley Road at what is now called Pippenhall.

The Sergeant received as wages 8s 8d at 2d per week. Two bushels of salt were bought to make the serfs' porridge for 10d and the pot in which to make it cost 1d. Digging the new garden and planting beans cost 8s and a shovel was obtained for 1d. The manorial courts dealt with minor offences and fines for certain rights such as inheriting one's father's lands. Brewing of beer seemed to cause many problems, as did trespass. Failure to keep water-courses also caused repeated complaints to the manorial court. Members of a family named Wolnoth of Wiklond regularly appeared as culprits in court and were fined a few pence for each offence.

Another series of manorial documents for Eltham and Eltham Mandeville for the later years of the 14th century have survived. That for the year 1370 in the reign of Edward III is particularly interesting for it tells of the enclosure of certain fields with hedges made of faggots. One such field was "Brandonshawe." Now it is owned by the London Borough of Greenwich and is allotment gardens - Pippenhall Allotments. The hedge on the western edge of the allotments has been dated by naturalists as being approximately 600 years old. The faggots were put around the field in 1370, they rooted and the hedge is still there, over 600 years later, a living relic of medieval Eltham.

The accounts show the influence of the Royal Parks for there is reference to loss of rents due to enclosure of land into the new park. New hedges were being made around the parks and John de Beverley, the Parker, received 3d per day in wages. Crops in 1370 were the same as in 1322 but now sheep were also mentioned for 286 fleeces of wool were obtained. Another 48 fleeces were taken from sheep that had died of murrain. The "Black Death" reached our shores in 1349 and decimated the population and no doubt Eltham suffered like the rest of England. The shortage of labour meant that arable farming was no longer viable so landlords turned to sheep rearing to maintain their income. Wool was a valuable commodity in trade with Europe and England's prosperity was based on it. Horses and cattle had also died of murrain. A dove-cot supplied pigeons for the table and the birds were fed vetch during the winter. Again, expenditure on ploughs was very high - £7 4s.

Pippenhall Allotments, Bexley Road showing
ancient hedge, 1989   S.F.C.

The 14th and 15th centuries saw the Crown consolidating its estates. Meanwhile the Well Hall estate was emerging as a separate entity. Passing through several owners, it came, in the second half of the 15th century, into the hands of the Ropers, a prominent Kentish family with estates around Canterbury. With the demise of the last of the Plantagenets, Richard III, on Bosworth Field in 1485 and the rise of the Tudor dynasty, most of Eltham was in the hands of two landlords, the Crown and the Ropers. These were to dominate Eltham for the next two centuries.

THE OWNERS OF WELL HALL 1436-1731

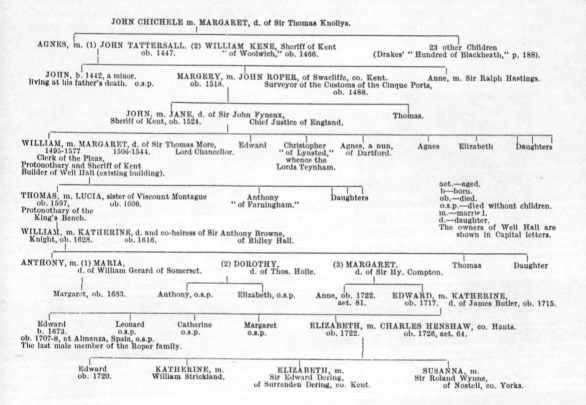

NOT SO MERRY ENGLAND ?

Tudor England is characterised as a country in political, religious and agrarian turmoil. It is pictured in the folklore tradition as "Merrie England." Eltham's local evidence contains elements of both.

At Eltham Palace can be seen the Great Hall (built 1479-1482) with its magnificent hammer-beam roof. This is the main survivor of a great complex of buildings which, throughout the 16th century, dominated that part of Eltham's skyline. Three and four storey Royal Apartments were built on the orders of Henry VII overlooking the western part of the moat and with distant views of the City of London. The Great Court, inside the wide moat, and the Green Court outside it, formed irregular quadrangles of clustered buildings. Furthest from the Great Hall's grandeur were such noxious necessities as the laundry and slaughterhouse. A plan of the Palace made by the surveyor, John Thorpe, has survived but there is no known illustration from that century.

The Great Hall of Eltham Palace, built 1479   J.S.

The Palace served as a royal nursery because the air of Eltham was considered to be healthy. The three deer parks attracted royal visitors for hunting. Eltham Palace was also regularly used by the King and Court during their progresses around southern England in the first half of the sixteenth century. Henry VII and his Queen spent much time at Eltham. His builders worked for much of 1500 constructing a new bridge and repairing the bakery and lodges.

Henry VIII kept Christmas at Eltham Palace in 1515 and 1525. In 1520 a large new chapel was built for him. He was again in residence in the summer of 1532 and in 1534, accompanied then by Queen Anne Boleyn and the infant Princess Elizabeth. Mary Tudor came in 1556, just for a fortnight. She appointed Sir Henry Jerningham as her Steward of the Palace. He was already Captain of the Queen's Guard. The chaplain he appointed died the following year and was buried in the parish church. Elizabeth I came briefly in 1559, 1560, 1568, 1569, 1576, 1581, 1596, 1597, 1598, 1601 and 1602. Often, the Churchwardens' accounts include a reference to the church bells being rung in welcome.

"Itm paid for drinke when the quene cam thorow the Towne."

The visits are also documented in the State Papers of her reign in the Public Record Office. She appointed Sir Christopher Hatton as Keeper of the Great Park. Lord Cobham held this office in 1591 and Sir Thomas Walsingham in 1600, just as Henry Skillman had under her grandfather. Very gradually, throughout the century, the Palace at Eltham was deserted in favour of "Placentia" at Greenwich.

In compensation for the use of local resources by the presence of the Court, Henry VII, in 1492, gave 38 acres of royal land scattered around Eltham to the poor of the parish. This was

"towards payment of their fifteenths in consideration of so great a portion of the land in the parish belonging to the Crown."

The inhabitants of 1674 said that "from time immemorial" (from 1492) a field adjacent to the Horne Parke, and other fields known as Blunts Croft, Molescroft, Barber's Shaw etc. had been held for the use and benefit of the poor. The present "Fifteenpenny Fields Almshouses" in Blunts Road. are derived from the benevolence of Henry VII, a monarch more generally famed for miserliness.

"The Statutes of Eltham," drawn up by Cardinal Wolsey as Lord Chancellor in 1526 provide a detailed insight into life at the Court of Henry VIII and the behaviour of servants as well as courtiers.

"Dinner shall be at ten, supper at four." "The proper officers are, between six and seven every morning, to make up the fire and put fresh straw on the floor of His Majesty's Privy Chamber."

"Master Cooks shall employ such scullions as shall not go about naked, nor lie about all night before the kitchen fire."

It is particularly stressed that servants were to be,

"discreet, keeping all things secret as shall be done or said in the King's Chamber."

Perhaps morals in regard to property and possessions were also lacking, since it was thought necessary to include the injunction that,

"His Highness' attendants are not to steal any locks or keys, tables, cupboards or other furniture out of gentlemen's houses where they go to visit."

Cardinal Wolsey stayed, as Chancellor, in the houses just outside the Palace moat correctly called "My Lord Chancellor, His Lodgings," now sadly suburbanised into 34-38 Courtyard. Sir Thomas More, Lord Chancellor 1529-1535, was familiar with the Palace from earlier years. In 1499 he had brought the Dutch scholar, Erasmus, to visit the royal children.

It is to be supposed that during the King's visits to the Palace, Sir Thomas More visited Well Hall, the home of his daughter, Margaret and her husband, William Roper, a lawyer who had trained in More's household. The house stood within the existing moat. The surviving Tudor Barn, moat and garden walls could remind visitors to what is now known as The Pleasaunce, of the sixteenth century occupants of the Well Hall estate. Margaret More married William Roper in July, 1521 when she was 15 and he was in his mid twenties. She bore him 5 children before she died, aged 39, at Christmas in 1544. She had been educated in Latin and Greek by her father and their surviving correspondence during his imprisonment in the Tower of London was a comfort and support to him...... a sensitive insight into their personalities for historians, literature for students of the English Language and inspiration for the pious. His final note included "Farewell, my dear child and pray for me, and I shall for you and your friends that we may merrily meet in heaven."

The More and Roper families, and indeed their entire households, suffered for their loyalty to the Roman Catholic faith. Sir Thomas More was brought to trial on 1st July 1535 and executed on 6th July 1535. In 1544 John Ireland, the Roper's chaplain at Canterbury and at Well Hall from 1535, and John Larke, Rector of Chelsea from 1530 who had been confessor to Sir Thomas More, were martyred at Tyburn. Other less eminent or less ardent adherents of the old faith managed to survive the turbulent Reformation years by practising their religion in secret or, in Elizabeth I's reign, incurring financial rather than capital penalties. These included several generations of Ropers and their servants........."Old Bromhed" who died in 1603, was buried near the derelict chapel at Kidbrooke, being banned from the Parish Churchyard. Others to suffer were Humphrey Eyton, John Doonse, and some members of the Twist family.

"My Lord Chancellor, his lodgings" viewed from the Moat Bridge, 1989

S.F.C.

From the evidence of wills, from the Churchwardens'
accounts which survive from 1554 and the parish registers
which exist from 1583 we can glean glimpses of how more
ordinary villagers lived their lives in Tudor Eltham. It is
evident from these sources that, during the 16th century, some
of the people of Eltham were in Royal service. There were
trumpeters, like Thomas and Francis Reston. Mistress Anne
Twist, a relation of Eltham's Vicar in 1585, was Queen
Elizabeth I's laundress. Other Eltham tradesmen would have
supplied the needs of the Court at such times as it was
present and possibly used this to advertise their wares, much
as the shops of the village near Balmoral all claim to sell
their goods "By Royal Appointment" today. Some of Eltham's
richer families had financial interests, second homes or
businesses in the City of London.

Extract from Churchwardens' Accounts of 1599

It is clear that the influence of the Palace declined rapidly in the second half of the century.

However, the bellringers dutifully welcomed Queen Elizabeth on her infrequent visits

John and Agnes Passey, whose surname survives in Passey Place made their wills in 1509 and 1512 and had them witnessed by Robert Makerell, the Vicar. John Passey was a yeoman porter to King Henry VIII and a brass memorial to him was embedded in the floor of the church. Another will, made in 1516, shows Eltham Church had altars, shrines and images of Our Lady of Pity, Our Lady in the Chancel, St. John, St. Katherine, St. Nicholas and the somewhat obscure St. Cithe, as well as a rood loft. Henry Oldcastle's will specifically requests that his body be buried before the altar of St. Nicholas under a stone with his picture on it holding the words "Jesu fili Dei miserere mei" (Jesus, son of God, have pity on me). There was also to be a representation of the Trinity. An idea of Henry Oldcastle's home is gained from his other bequests....

"a paire of blankets and a pint pot, a brasse pot and a ketall, napkins, two towels, tablecloths, platters, candlesticks, snuffers, a featherbed and a doublet of black damask."

This will was proved at Dartford on July 23rd 1518.

Wills often blend the sacred with the earthly mud of the local roads. Repair of the roads was a charitable community service. In May 1520 Henry Keightley's will made provision for his wife, Elizabeth, but also left specific instructions about the repair of the highway between Pope Street (New Eltham) and the town (Eltham) "and to none other highway nore by laynes." It is appropriate that there is now a street name "Keightley Drive" commemorating him. Thomas Parker's will of 1521 was witnessed by Philip Carrock, the Vicar of this date. When the will was executed in 1523, his widow, Mary, was provided for and the surplus was spent equally on dirges and masses and on the mending of highways. John and Lettice Collynson or Collenson made their wills in 1534 and 1541. They, too, were much concerned about the repair of

"the highway between Wyatt Elm (New Eltham) and the towne and between Westende Cross and the towne where most need is or shall be."

He leaves his best doublet to his servant, Thomas Metcalf. She leaves to an in-law, Julyan Brikett, two cows, one mare, five silver spoons and "all my gowns of good stuff." In 1555 the Footscray Road must have still been unsatisfactory for Richard Maynard made provision

"to repair the way to Wiotts Elm, to begin where the old causeway was made."

Repairs at "Wyatts Elm?" The Collenson Will did not bear this expense in 1974. (Re-building of Avery Hill Road bridge)   *J.K.C.*

William Lambarde, famed as the author of the "Perambulation of Kent" made a will in 1576 benefiting residents of Eltham who were eligible to apply for admission to his Queen Elizabeth Hospital (almshouses) at Greenwich...the first such foundation established by a Protestant. The people of Eltham, like the other inmates, would have to pray willingly twice a day for,

"God to save his Church Universal, our gracious Queen Elizabeth, her nobility and councellors, the Master of the Rolls, the Company of Drapers and the whole clergy and commonality of this realm."

They should not be people who "hath longe dwelte in popish idolatry and superstition." Nor should they "play at dice,coits or shove-groat." Thomas Roper's will of 1578 left money derived from four acres of the old East Field. Eventually this helped to provide the site of the 19th century National School and 22 houses in what is now Roper Street. Even as we shop in the late 20th century High Street, we are reminded of 16th century benefactors by the street names Passey Place and Roper Street.

With the decline of the Palace there had been a growth in the commercial, trading and farming life of Tudor Eltham. During political, religious and agricultural troubles it appears the majority of Eltham's residents simply attempted to earn an uneventful living. Most lived in the High Street which ran eastwards from its junction with the highway to Woolwich (now Sherard Road) as it does today. They took their water from wells in their yards and gardens and deposited their sewage in adjacent cesspits. The parish registers record all who were baptised, married or buried irrespective of social position. There were wealthy and influential families like the Allees and the Elliots. There were also ordinary working families of bricklayers, tilers, carpenters, potters, lime-workers, blacksmiths and labourers. From the 16th century onwards it is possible to know the names of even the poorest. John Spenser, for example, was paid to dig a sawpit at Weston Green (Eltham Green) in 1554 and to saw a tree trunk into planks to mend the bridge over the Quaggy.

Such people and their families worshipped in the parish church of St. John the Baptist. They sent "oulde Thomas Adeane " to buy a "new Graylle" in 1555, bought frankincense by the pound weight and were ministered to by celibate clergy. In 1558 they employed a painter from London to repaint the Rood and the statues of Mary and John at a cost of eight shillings. Philip Carrack, Vicar 1521-8 had a housekeeper called Joan Garnett. John Carnecke, Vicar 1568-76, left money for a church clock. In 1985 descendants of James Twiste, Vicar 1585-89 contacted Eltham in search of information on their ancestry. The resulting story further illustrated the inter-relationship of leading families in Elizabethan Eltham for the Twistes and the Allees had intermarried. The church presided over by Vicar John Ford (Fourde), 1589-1627 would have been different in character from that known at the start of the century to Rev. Thurston Anderton. Ford was a bigoted and vengeful type of Protestant, frequently at odds with the closet-Catholics of the Roper household, his northern neighbours.

There was religious zeal for the re-conversion of England as well as territorial greed in the motivation for the very real threat of invasion from Spain in 1588. A beacon was set up on Shooters Hill, the parish's highest point. This would have been visible for miles around and therefore able to transmit a warning. A muster of the City of London's troops had been called on Blackheath in April/May 1585, at which 4,000-5,000 soldiers were encamped whilst Her Majesty was at Greenwich Palace. Many of them "dressed themselves with scarves and feathers." To such musters Eltham parish sent its tiny contingent of men under the constable, Bromhed. Nicholas Spilsted and Jeffery Starbuck, for example were provided with some armour and pikes by the parish. It is perhaps fortunate for the defence of the realm that the Armada was defeated at sea without the opportunity to land efficient troops. Eltham, like every other parish, had archery butts where all able-bodied adult men were supposed to train weekly. These were situated approximately where Strongbow Road, Strongbow Crescent and Archery Road are now. Eltham's churchwardens had supervised the setting up of a maypole in 1562 and there was, doubtless, some similar rejoicing in the Autumn of 1588 at the defeat of the Armada.

In 1593 an Eltham resident, Ingram Friser, was involved in the murder of playwright, Christopher Marlowe, in a tavern in Deptford. A volatile mixture of politics, religion and espionage were involved in this incident.

Approximately a third of Eltham parish, throughout the 16th century, was occupied by the three Royal deer parks, Great, Middle and Horn, each surrounded by its "park pale" or high fence. Sir William Roper had also enclosed a considerable area eastwards from Well Hall. The remaining land area of Eltham was divided into an apparently haphazard patchwork of small fields, surrounded by hedges and used for mixed arable and stock-rearing farming. The street names Beanshaw, Domonic Drive and Edgebury commemorate field names of the Elizabethan era but are not entirely in their original locations. By 1605 there were two windmills, one near the north west corner of the parish (near the present "Welcome Inn" Public House) and the other in the vicinity of the present Warren Golf Course.

The estimated population of Eltham in 1600 was 600. The population had more than doubled since the early Middle Ages but, due to the enclosure of the parks, the area under cultivation had been halved since those times. Crafts and commerce had, of necessity, to be added to farming, if the population was to prosper. Literacy was therefore increasingly desirable.

As Eltham moved towards the next century the villagers would perhaps have been more concerned with the building of a school, apparently adjacent to the church, where Goodman Wyborne would continue teaching their children.

"paid to Mr. Elliot for moving of timber from the common to the scoole hous"

"Recefed of Mr. Hewe Miller the xii of September toward the billding of the cembne (chimney) in the skowlehowes xxd."

As William Lambarde wrote " It is happy for the state when each man having first laid in a stock of general knowledge, will thus be content...."

PARLIAMENT AND PESTILENCE

Histories of our country and county in the 17th century tell of plague and pestilence, pikemen and parliamentary petitions, Papists and Puritans.

In 1605, while the Gunpowder Plot was being hatched, King James I was ordering his commissioners to enquire into landownership and occupiers in Eltham. Fortunately, the survey still survives in the Public Record Office. This survey suggests that about 1000 acres of Eltham were then woodland, 1300 acres park or pasture and about 700 acres were under cultivation.

Placing the survey's evidence together with personal details discovered from parish records and wills, it is possible to gain an impression of the people of the village of Eltham at the start of the 17th century. Royalty and their attendant courtiers visited the Palace only for brief hunting expeditions. Royal proteges like the French physician, Theodore Mayerne and the Dutch painter Anthony Van Dyke were granted sinecures or lodgings in the vicinity of the old Palace by the King. It is doubtful if they mixed much with the village people. By the provisions of the 1601 Poor Law a stranger passing through on a journey or staying briefly, perhaps at harvest time, had to carry a certificate from his own parish agreeing to take him back should he need public assistance through illness or unemployment. From such visitors, Eltham people learned of happenings in the rest of Europe.

1626 "two poore women with three children...coming with a pass out of the low countryes."

1629 "paid to a poor man that had his tongue cut out by the Turks 1s 11d"

1666 "4 ffrenchmen and women with certificates for relief being in great distress 2s."

The rich and poor, and an increasing number of yeomen-tradespeople who fell somewhere between those categories, led inter-dependent lives still closely tied to the effects of weather and the frequency of epidemics. Major adjustments were being made in the local economy as dependence on royal patronage gave way to local trade and agriculture. Apart from the Roper family, who remained at Well Hall until the close of the century, the surnames found in 1600 differ greatly from those of 1700. It was a changing population.

Plagues raged in Eltham in 1603, 1625 and 1646. Fifty four Eltham residents died in 1603, 18 certainly of the Plague, of whom Sarah, daughter of John Grace, was the first on 17th August. The last burial of a plague victim was on the following January 13th. It seems the poor suffered more than the rich though all lived in conditions which we would regard as insanitary. Attempts were made to control the pestilence by isolating the victims. Elizabeth (Bess) Bevens and Goody Hassal were Eltham's midwives of the 1620's. They were also paid, in 1625, "fore to looke to those that had the plague." Arrangements were made for "putten of crosses on the doores of the houses that weare infected of the plague" and "the house that Hassall dwelte in" was in use for five months as a "peste house", or as we might term it ...an isolation ward. The bell tolled in Eltham for 60 deaths in that year but only a handful are listed as plague victims. Again the first casualty occurred in the summer. In 1646 there were 36 burials in Eltham churchyard of whom 7 are specifically listed as having died of plague. That year it was epidemic from July 25th to September 19th only. It had apparently been brought by its first victim, Sarah, daughter of Mr. Barber of London. Eltham appears to have escaped London's Great Plague in 1665, perhaps by a less hospitable attitude to travellers and visitors. One man was buried at Weston Green (Eltham Green) and not brought into the town, as a precaution.

Commercial links with London increased during the 17th century. Some of the church bells were recast in 1610 and in 1618. They took the Great Bell to Mr. Morrte in Whitechapel and had to pay tolls at London Bridge and at "Allgate." This 1618 errand to "Howensditch" took three days in all. Children placed as apprentices by the parish sometimes gained work with London merchants. More usually, poor apprentice children were placed with local people...yeomen, shoemakers, carpenters, butchers, bakers or woodmen.

If we had walked into Eltham in the first decade of the 17th century we might have met the Bremington family, weavers with a side-line in honey from the bees in hives in their backyard. They also had a large barn where tramps and travellers were often allowed a night's rest. We might have met young Dorrite Mumbe playing outside her parent's home in the Courtyard and later mourned her accidental death caused by "Mr. Roper's windmill." We could, if the year was 1608, have seen "Old Glozier slain removing his privy house."

Rear view of the old Castle Tavern, c. 1880   *E.S.C.*

In central Eltham, where "The Castle" public house now stands, lived Hugh Miller, one of Eltham's richest townsfolk and "lately one of the Quene's footmen." He farmed about 50 acres in Eltham. His house had three storeys with 21 chambers and contained wainscot, leather chairs, books, tables, beds, a paire of old virginalls, brasse pots and wall hangings. The complete contents are listed in an inventory taken on his death in 1615. The total value of his goods was £122 18s 4d. In his will he leaves the goods that his wife brought as a dowry to her and the rest to his son, Francis, to sell.

Houses in more contemporary styles were added during the century to the High Street frontages. Sherard House was built in a fashionable Dutch style in 1634 and fortunately survived into the era of photography. Also in 1634 the "skole house" was improved, too late to be enjoyed by "Old Wybourne" the first known Eltham schoolmaster, who died in abject poverty in 1637. The village had paid its Ship Money Tax in 1636 and paid George and William Jennings 3 shillings to carry the parish armour to the muster in April 1637. The Church Rate book of 1636 suggests that there were nine large landowning households, 45 commonplace ones, 32 households liable to pay less than 2/6d and 9 due to pay under one shilling. A stone dated 1653 may be noted on 150 High Street, recalling a previous house of that date which stood on the site.

The stone plaques set into the gabled premises
give the dates of three re-buildings, 1988   *J.K.C.*

These townspeople of Eltham regularly celebrated the failure of the Gunpowder Plot with bell-ringing on the anniversary. By the will of Richard Slynn, former Park-Keeper of Horn Park, from 1642, a public Protestant sermon was to be preached and bread given to the poor on every November 5th. A whipping post was installed in 1619 for the punishment of wrong-doers and the stocks were repaired in 1642.

The 1605 survey has evidence of only one inn, The George, situated where no. 78 High Street is now. During the 17th century "The Castle," "The White Hart" and "The Carpenters Arms" were added. Nathaniel and Tamsin Mercer married in 1616, took apprentices into their vintners business and had their initials on their Trade Tokens for "The Castle" in 1649. The need for such local token coinage reflects the monetary problems of the nation at the time. This was caused by the Civil War and the fact that no coin smaller than a silver 3d piece was legally minted during the years 1649-1660. Shops and inns throughout the country had to provide local equivalents to small change - their trade tokens. Richard Green built and opened "The Carpenters Arms" in 1666 soon after receiving £60 for timber work in the church in that year. Its successor stood at 162-164 Eltham High Street until 1986.

The Carpenters Arms Public House prior to demolition in 1986   *S.F.C.*

The County of Kent as a whole was inclined to the Royalist view in the Civil War. Robert Devereux, Earl of Essex and Commander of the Parliamentary Army, died at Eltham House (as the Palace was then described) in September 1646. His office was taken by Sir Thomas Fairfax, under the overall command of Oliver Cromwell. A Puritan attempt to ban the celebration of Christmas in Canterbury in 1647 led to a petition to Parliament from the people of Kent, who then planned to gather at Rochester in Spring 1648 and proceed to Blackheath and London, as had so many previous rebellions. Lord General Fairfax was sent to disperse the "Petitioners" with 7,000 horse and foot soldiers. These were billeted in and around Eltham for a few nights and then passed on in pursuit of fleeing "Petitioners."

The poorer people of Eltham, together with the visiting soldiers "tore down the fences that enclosed the Royal Parks, killed the deer, laid waste the gardens and pleasure ground, and ransacked the Palace." Perhaps the deer bones and antlers discovered in large numbers when Blann Close was built, near the site of the former Keeper's Lodge of Middle Park date from this time. There are reports of Palace tapestries being used as rugs and carpets by poor villagers. Legend attributes the "Tudor" fireplaces in "The Greyhound" to this illegal dispersal of Palace artefacts. The first known view of Eltham Palace, a print by Peter Stent, survives from 1650. It shows a Gothic moated complex, outwardly undisturbed.

Badgers and foxes were trapped in 17th century Eltham, as in other rural parishes, rewards for their destruction being recorded in the Churchwardens' Accounts. In the decade starting in 1643 the number caught increased sharply. The royal parks were then available to the parishioners and perhaps people suffering from increasing poverty were claiming a reward for whatever could raise even a few pence.

P.J.

Castle Tokens

By July 1649 a more orderly situation had been imposed after the brief interlude. Colonel Nathaniel Rich rode in with Parliamentary troops to protect Royal property from the common people. Parliament had ordered the execution of the king but retained his lands for state use. Two years later the Colonel purchased much of the estate for himself. In the Autumn of 1649, a parliamentary survey was made, comparable to the Royal survey of 1605. The Lord Protector Cromwell was especially interested in the many trees growing in the three royal parks of Eltham which were then at suitable maturity to provide timber for ship-building in the dockyards at Deptford and Woolwich. The tree felling must have caused considerable alteration in the local landscape. Orders were issued to fell 730 oak, elm and ash trees. By an Act of 17th July 1649 the felling was permitted to continue at a similar rate until 1657, and it probably did. John Evelyn wrote in his diary on 26th April 1656,

> "I went to see his majestie's house at Eltham, both
> palace and chapell in miserable ruins, and the
> woods and parks destroyed by Rich the Rebell."

There is no way of telling what Eltham's people felt about the execution of Charles I.....landlord to many of them.....in January 1649. It would have been unwise to voice an opinion, still less put it in writing even if they were literate, which many were not. The lists of

> "persons relieved in regard of their great charge
> and the dearenesis of provision and scarcitie of
> work"

lengthen considerably in the years following 1649. High living costs and unemployment are nothing new. In April 1649 "at a public Vestrie" the parishioners implemented Parliament's rulings forbidding anyone to receive lodgers in their houses.

The Lord Protector's strict Puritan laws extended even to regulation of games, which were not to be permitted on a Sunday. Seven Eltham lads were fined for playing cricket "on ye Lord's Daye" in May 1654. They were Francis Clayford, Edward Layton, John Poole, Will Ffoye, Will and Thomas Starbuck and the Widow Roode's son. It is one of the earliest references to the game of cricket. Needy children, possibly orphaned in the Civil war, were cared for at parish expense in the 1650's much as they had been before. In due course such children were again locally apprenticed to husbandmen and farmers, a "taylor," a nailer and a wigmaker or in Deptford to a gunner and mariner, or in Greenwich to an oarsmaker.

The Vicar, Richard Owen, was dismissed from his office on suspicion of Royalist sympathies. William Overton replaced him from 1646-58 and supervised Samuel Farnaby as he plastered and whitened the church. However, the parish register lists Richard Owen as "Vicar of Eltham" when he married Amy Kidwell on 6th January 1654/55. He often preached in the Library of John Evelyn's house at Sayes Court, Deptford. John Lilburne died in Eltham in 1657, having lived the final years of his exciting life, quietly as a Quaker, on a 40 shilling parliamentary pension. Clement Hobson, Vicar from 1658-1726 was a local version of the "Vicar of Bray," managing to keep his head and vocation through many changes of religious and political fashion. Other clergy thrown out of office attempted to support themselves and their families by setting up as schoolmasters. Caleb Trenchfield was licensed to preach in Rochester Diocese, to which Eltham belonged. A sermon he preached in Lee in 1662 was supposed to have contained "dangerous matters." He had served as Rector of Chipstead, Surrey, during the Commonwealth but was a schoolmaster in Eltham in 1664. The Greene and Roper families were fined repeatedly through the century as "recusants." Others were similarly punished; those later in the century possibly being religious refugees from Europe.

Church and State were interconnected in the 17th century. The bells at Eltham were rung at the Restoration of Charles II in 1660 and at every anniversary of his Coronation. The church building was, however, as insecure as its personnel. In 1667, whilst building a new chapel, insufficient scaffolding was used to make the rest of the edifice secure. The nave roof fell and the severe damage that resulted cost £98 5s to repair and was paid to John Guy, a bricklayer. Similar large payments were made to a carpenter, glazier, locksmith, tiler and other craftsmen. The medieval building was frequently repaired and altered in brick for the remainder of its existence.

The intended church extension had been commissioned by Sir John Shaw, a wealthy banker who had aided Charles II with loans during his exile in the Commonwealth years. In partial recompense he had been given a long lease on the Manor of Eltham. Members of the Shaw family occupied the position of Eltham's "Squire" for the succeeding century. The first Sir John Shaw, having decided that the original Palace was uninhabitable in 1660, ordered the building of a fine mansion designed by Hugh May, an associate of Sir Christopher Wren.

This building we now know as the club house of the Royal Blackheath Golf Club, off Court Road. The new house, completed in 1664, was soon graced with family portraits painted by the renowned Peter Lely. Yet even this richest of Eltham's families did not have the clear tap water and drainage facilities which the late 20th century resident takes for granted. Their fresh water was piped in hollowed tree trunks to this new mansion from the conduit head which can still be seen in the meadow behind Holy Trinity Church in Southend Crescent. John Evelyn wrote in his diary on 14th July 1664,

"Thence to Eltham to see Sir John Shaw's new house now building, the place is pleasant, if not too wett but the house is not well contrived, especially the roofe and dormers too low pitched, and kitchens where the cellars should be. The orangerie and Aviarie handsome, and a very large plantation about it."

The Conduit Head   P.J.

Like his poorer fellow parishioners Sir John Shaw had to pay his rates and the new Hearth Tax, a tax on fireplaces. From such evidence an impression of Eltham can be built up to compare and contrast with the picture discerned from the 1636 Church Rate. It appears that in 1664 there were 14 empty houses in the parish and of the 155 inhabited houses 83 had only one or two hearths. 57 homes were so poor as to be "not chargeable." Only 14 homes had four hearths, ten had five and nine had six hearths each. Only six houses had more than six hearths.

New farms were established where there had been royal deer parks and old established farms continued to exist. The newer fields tended to be larger, to have more regular, rectangular shapes and to have less colourful names. At Southend lived Judge William Wythens, associate of the notorious Judge Jefferies, who presided over the "Bloody Assize" which, in 1685, decimated the youth of the West Country after the ill-fated Monmouth Rebellion. Judge Wythens probably approved of the Cage built by the parish in 1687 at a cost of £6 15s 4d for the containment of minor criminals. He supported the penal system which maintained a gallows on Shooters Hill where the bodies of the executed were left hanging as an example to others. Samuel Pepys complained that the gallows was a "filthy sight." John Evelyn describes William Wythens attending a wedding and talking "much beneath the gravity of Judges." At Southend, Eltham, clay pipes dating from about 1610-1680 have been found on Wythens' land. We may imagine those residents who could afford the new luxury, tobacco, freshly imported from the New World.... an unexplored continent of wonders. The name of Eltham was carried to the New World by a certain James Smallwood in 1684. There it described 75 acres of land in Charles County, Maryland, a district still noted for tobacco growing.

The Philipot Almshouses were established by the will of Thomas Philipot in 1680 and building commenced on a High Street site, just west of Blunts Road, in 1694. Small red-brick cottages were provided for the deserving elderly poor of Eltham and Chislehurst. Philipot also left land in New Eltham to provide an endowment for Clare College, Cambridge where he had studied. This explains the street names Clare Corner and Cambridge Green.

When Gregory Chalkin died at the end of the 17th century he left, among other things.....

"in the best chamber, beds, chairs, stools and boxes, in the chamber over the kitchen, one feather bed, in the garats,

3 bedds,
19 pare of sheets
5 horse harness, 3 carts, 2 plows
a pare of harrows
6 cowes, 67 sheepe, 6 hoggs
wheat, oats, clover, hay, dung and other things in his barn,"

to a total of £476 19s 11d.

By the listed goods and chattels and taking into account the high rate of inflation during the 17th century it can be seen that he was less wealthy than Hugh Miller had been. Nevertheless, he was comfortably off by comparison with most of his neighbours.

In 1600 there were more deer than people in the parish of Eltham, but by 1700 the deer had been slaughtered by the local populace and the grazing grounds were under cultivation.

Despite the execution of the king, eleven years under alleged Parliamentary rule, a "Glorious Revolution" in 1688 and an increase in farming there seemed to be just as many poor inhabitants leading a hand to mouth existence. Eltham's Royal links were severed. It was just one more little village on the road into Kent.

Southend House as refurbished, 1990   *S.F.C.*

ELTHAM STREET 1605

Key

1 Thomas Barnham
2 Elizabeth Petley
3 Thos & Phillip Rolfe
4 Vicarage
5 Parsonage Barn
6 Parish Church
7 Robert Younge
8 John Kettle
9 Anne Twist
10 Walter Parry
11 Phillip Stubbes
12 Henry Birde
13 John Alee
14 William Eliot
15 Edward Borie
16 John Harrison
17 Hugh & Henry Stubbes
18 Toby & Thomas Stubbes
19 Robert Younge
20 Hugh Edwards
21 Heires of Manning & Eliot
22 Joseph Bremington
23 James Dowley & others
24 John & Roger Harvie
25 Heires of Manning
26 Sir William Wythens

27 Francis Reston
28 Henry Manning
29 Thomas Martin
30 Francis Reston
31 Michell Bonner
32 Anne Twist
33 Elizabeth Baker
34 Hugh Miller
35 Adam Holloway
36 William Swallow
37 John Alee
38 Thomas Sampson
39 George Clarke
40 Ardenn Moore
41 John Hodgkin
42 John Layton
43 William Mumbye
44 Nicholas Spelst
45 John Stubbes
46 Francis Reston
47 The George
48 Thomas Batt
49 Ingram Freeser
50 John Sherlock
51 John Newington
52 Thomas & Phillip Rolfe

44

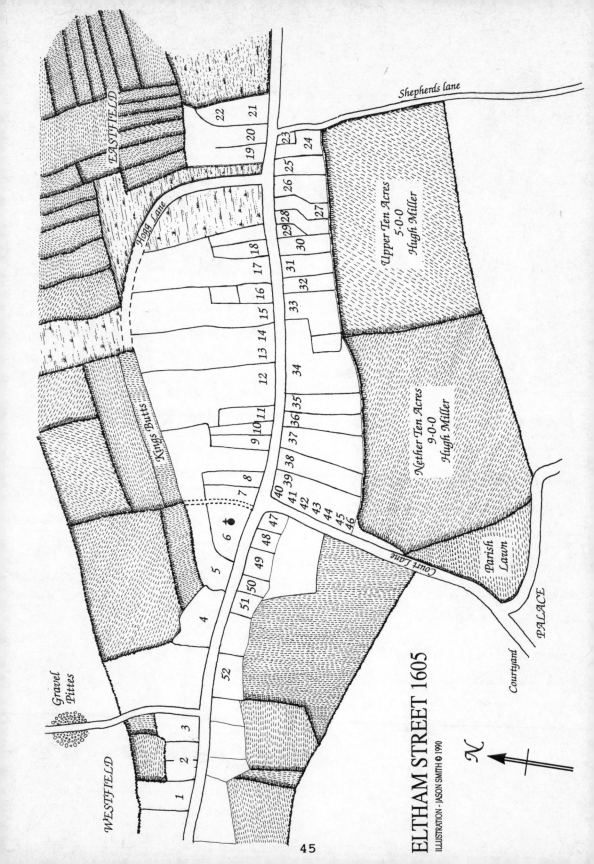

ELTHAM STREET 1605

ILLUSTRATION - JASON SMITH © 1990

John Gregory Shaw, son of Sir John Shaw, Bart. and Martha, his Lady, was born 25th July and baptised 22nd August 1756

Mrs. Felicia Burton, wife of Philip Burton Esq. died 30th January 1791 aged 78 years.

Sarah Guilliard, daughter of Nicholas, the perukemaker, and Sarah (Taylor) died aged 2 years on 22nd September 1786

Samuel James, a negro, was baptised 28th July 1753.

John Brier or Fryer, son of Sir John Shaw's carter, was baptised 12th February 1758

Elizabeth Smith, widow, servant to Philip Burton Esq., died December 26th 1790 aged 40 years.

Mary Smith from Mottingham, died of the smallpox aged 14 years. 31st Jan. 1788

James, base-born son of Mary Wright, James Williams of Pippinhall ye supposed father, was baptised on 11th March 1741.

ELEGANCE AND POVERTY

Eltham may have become just one more little village on the road from London into Kent by 1700 but it certainly did not lie dormant in the next century, more a case of gathering its resources together to meet the coming industrial age. Crown and Court had all but forgotten this village which had served the former Royal Palace, even leasing its manorial rights to a London banker.

However, Eltham could not totally forget the City of London which, after all, was only eight miles away, a distance not too difficult to cover in a day, even in those times, by stage coach. Contemporary opinion has it that Eltham was becoming a semi-urban area populated by retired members of the leisured classes, lawyers, merchants and officers from the Army and Navy. Daniel Defoe said, in 1726,

"It is now a pleasant town, very handsomely built, full of good houses and many families of rich citizens inhabit here. So it is here they bring a great deal of good company with them. Also, abundance of ladies of very good fortunes dwell here."

Such writers, of course, ignore the existence of the ubiquitous poor, but the class divisions, inherent in the society of the time were nowhere more apparent than in what we know as the High Street. This main street saw a variety of buildings, from town houses such as Queenscroft (146 Eltham Hill) and Cliefden (97 High Street), both still with us today, the latter somewhat disguised as shops and offices, to cottages, almshouses, the obligatory workhouse and several inns. The "Greyhound" is still with us today in its much restored 18th century premises and others like the "Chequers" and the "Castle" survive but in more recent buildings. Some are only names lost in the realms of history - The Star, The White Swan and The Black Horse. Many buildings were built of brick and tiles (see Queenscroft for a beautifully restored example) but others were weather-boarded in the typical Kentish fashion and timber framed. The other important building was the much repaired parish church, situated at the western end of the main street, with vicarage and tithe barn close by.

In 1733, the Roper's estate at Well Hall was sold to Sir Gregory Page. He demolished the building within the moated area and built a new house. This stood between the moat and what is now Well Hall Road. The site is now part of the lawns at the entrance to the Pleasaunce. The Tudor structure to the north of the moat survived as farm buildings and now forms the Tudor Barn Restaurant. The Great Hall of Eltham Palace had also degenerated into a barn.

Although we are now used to regular commuter transport to London and elsewhere, even in the 18th century it was not unknown for regular coach services to pass through the town. The main Maidstone to London road which became part of the Turnpike system in the early 1780's passed along Eltham's main street and saw as varied and colourful set of travellers as many a modern thoroughfare. Wool, cattle, sheep, hops and continental imports such as silks and toys were conveyed on a variety of goods vehicles from two wheeled carts to four wheeled wagons. How far we've come with the Sainsbury's container lorries! Passengers were carried by a similar variety of vehicles, from coaches both public and private, chariots, chaises, hearses, to mail coaches and post coaches which also carried foreign mail.

SIR THOMAS MOORES HOUSE, WELL HALL, ELTHAM

Well Hall House, built c. 1735, demolished c. 1935 as seen from Well Hall Road

E.S.C.

The stage coach service improved as the century went on, becoming more reliable as regards timetable and speed. Speeds increased from four miles to seven miles an hour by the end of the century. Their added advantage was that they did not need to stop or slow down for the tollgates. That a more local service was also available is illustrated by various advertisements surviving from newspapers of the time. The Kentish Gazette records, in June 1768, that the Maidstone and Malling Stage Coach went to London and back twice weekly via Eltham. The Maidstone Journal, in 1786, shows a weekly winter service and a more frequent summer service, both of which called at Eltham. Wilke's Directory of 1793 shows Eltham as having two coaches daily to the Golden Cross Inn at Charing Cross and one daily to the Spread Eagle Inn in Gracechurch Street in the City. A daily cart service and a twice weekly wagon service from Eltham to Southwark are also mentioned. Besides improving access for Eltham residents to London and the rest of Kent the prosperity of the High Street's inns was assured.

Eltham Lodge viewed from the south, c. 1985   *J.K.C.*

The 18th century was a time of vast social differences the "rich" and the "poor" lived, if not side by side, at least both within the parish of Eltham. The Shaw family were the Lords of the Manor, living at Eltham Lodge. The house has been described as "an outstanding example of early Restoration domestic design" and was one of the prototypes of a new style in England developed in the late 17th and early 18th centuries.

Sir John Shaw, the first baronet, had 11 children by two marriages (several descendants survive today) and it was the fourth baronet, also Sir John Shaw, who oversaw the modernisation of the Lodge in 1752-1755. In a survey conducted by John Holmes in 1749 for the fourth baronet's coming of age, the Shaw family were noted as holding 2184 acres of Crown Land, of which the park, farmland, house and garden comprised 215 acres, and 47 acres of freehold land elsewhere in the parish.

By the mid 1750's the social activities of the upper classes had become more elaborate, necessitating a less formal style of interior design. Balls, masquerades, musical parties and assemblies required a series of communal rooms running into each other. The popular way of achieving this was a circuit of reception rooms around a staircase, each room having a different colour scheme. Guests would therefore go up the stairs, through the different rooms, each offering a different form of entertainment and then down again.

Eltham Lodge required very little structural alteration but more extensive decoration to comply with these demands. This modernisation is reputed to have cost £10,000. There was a dining room, an innovation at that period, and a drawing room, to which the ladies retired after dessert. The gentlemen remained in the dining room, drinking and smoking, rejoining the ladies in the drawing room later in the evening. The library contained amusements for guests. These included souvenirs of the 4th baronet's grand tour, books, journals, games and scientific toys.

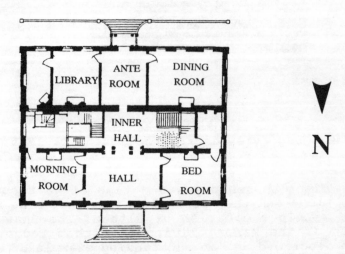

Plan of Eltham Lodge

Gardens were similarly designed on a circuit system, guests came out of the house and took a tour of the gardens, stopping to take tea in a temple or gazebo or view through a telescope at a rotunda. An estate document of 1780 describes substantial modernisation, including the building of a temple or pleasure house and creating a hot house and greenhouse for fruit growing. A similar document of 1805 describes the park as being 160 acres of rich meadow land with pleasure grounds and fish ponds. At this time also, the park was used for shooting, probably partridges. Entertainment was certainly not in short supply for the Shaw family and their guests.

A typical day in a country house of this period:-

9.30 a.m. Breakfast.

Gentlemen went shooting, fishing, played billiards.

Ladies walked in gardens, spent time in rooms, took a trip to town.

3.30 p.m. All change for dinner.

4 p.m. Dinner.

Ladies retired to drawing room.

Gentlemen played cards or billiards.

7 p.m. All gathered for tea and coffee, reading, writing, fortune telling, dancing, etc.

10 p.m. Supper.

Various pursuits as before supper.

12 midnight. All retired for the night.

♥♥♥♥♥♥   ♪♪♪♪   ♦♦♦♦♦♦   ♪♪♪♪♪   ♣♣♣♣♣♣   ♪♪♪♪♪   ♠♠♠♠♠♠

The fifth baronet left the Lodge in 1804 when the lease was given to Sir Edward Winnington and the Rev. Dr. Dodson who held it in trust for the Shaw family. In 1811 the fifth baronet renewed the lease for 28½ years and let out the Lodge and home farm and the rest of the estate at a profit. Several titled people leased the Lodge from the family between 1820-1838, Lord Wynford (1820), Lady Crewe (1821), Lord Rivers (1837), Francis Bruce (1838). The property had passed to the sixth baronet, Sir John Shaw on the death of his father in 1831. The sixth baronet was regarded the family's "black sheep."

Times became hard for the Shaw family after the sixth baronet (the black sheep) lost the family's fortune by his riotous living. He died in Paris in 1857. Family paintings and letters were sold to repay his debts and when the new parish church was built in 1875 there was no money to pay for the inclusion of the family vaults and memorials and so these were lost for ever. The family, however, continued to prosper. The tenth baronet, Sir John Best Shaw, succeeded to the title in 1984 and lives in Kent (1989) where he is active in church and community work.

The Shaw family of 18th century Eltham would have been well aware of the poor people in their locality "The poor are always with us," so the saying goes. The Parish Records provide much information on problems and poverty within the community. Examples from these records are quoted in this chapter. The first workhouse was built in Eltham in 1738/1739 using charitable funds. It was demolished in 1964 and replaced by the flats and parade of shops opposite the Fire Station. The three storied building, built at a cost of £313 by Mr. Wiggons, a carpenter of East Greenwich, of brick with a tiled roof contained a council room, parlour, kitchen, a large work room and a low ceilinged partitioned dormitory. Local gentlemen provided the fittings and furnishings, including cooking utensils, a Bible and Prayer Books, 39 yards of linen at 10½d a yard, 2 large coppers, a set of fire irons and 2 account books.

The building, commissioned in May 1738 was ready for occupation by April 1739 and "William Sharkey and his good wife" were the first to be "Chosen Master and Mistress." The workhouse provided accommodation for orphans, unemployed men and their families and the old. Any such paupers found within the parish boundaries were Eltham's responsibility. An example is Sam Onion who first appears in the records of the Overseers of the Poor as a carpenter, then a labourer, then an occupant of the workhouse. A sad decline in the fortunes of one man is recorded for posterity.

Who can tell how often his story was repeated in Eltham and other such areas in this period. Another example was Mary Vaughan, evicted by Bexley parish in the winter of 1748-1749 on to the Eltham Road so that "She gave birth to a female child in the parish of Eltham." Another occupant for the workhouse to admit, but one cannot help but wonder what became of the anonymous female child.

The Workhouse, 1738-1964   *E.S.C.*

The poor living in the workhouse were clothed by the parish according to the Account Books in 1740, "Pd for a petticoat and shift given to Jane Goodman, 4 shillings." Food was bought monthly in bulk. The 1740's diet included a side of bacon, "30 stone of beef meat, bread and flouer, a bushell of green peas" and a considerable quantity of cheap ale. The care by the workhouse authorities for the inhabitants lasted literally from the cradle to the grave. It is noted that cheap wooden coffins cost 2 shillings for a child's and 10 shillings for an adult's. There was a high mortality rate in the early days of the workhouse, averaging one death a month and sometimes more in winter.

1749 "Pd for a shroud and coffeen for Mrs. Roarbrite 10 shillings.

Pd for carrying her to the grave 5 shillings."

The richer inhabitants founded charities, some of which are still in existence today. Dame Sarah Pritchard, in 1707, financed the distribution of money to ten poor widows and maids. Mrs. Elizabeth Leggatt, in 1714, attempted to finance the teaching of the poor children of Eltham

> "to read, write and cast accounts" and "to be carefully and diligently instructed in the catechism, liturgy and doctrine of the Church of England."

Elizabeth Fearn and Mary Clapham, in 1711 and 1733, provided for distributions in money and in kind.

Some poorer folk obviously took to crime, R.R.C. Gregory's "The Story of Royal Eltham" (1909) details the activities of highwaymen on Shooters Hill, such as the one, in 1741, who robbed "a riding officer of the Excise" of about £20. Shades of Robin Hood and Dick Turpin for the romantically inclined. Parish funds were used to keep up the Cage wherein such offenders were incarcerated pending their transfer to Maidstone Jail.

Constables employed by the parish do not appear to have spent much time catching criminals, rather searching for the fathers of illegitimate offspring in order to make them pay for the upbringing of their bastards.

> 1724 "Expenses indeavouring to trace Edward Hartley who had a child given to him by Martha Barnes 16 shillings."

It has been seen that during this period Eltham had undergone many changes. A rapid growth in population, particularly in the second half of the century brought about the building of houses for both the gentry and the average villager and the development of services that both required. Life for the average villager was still based upon the agricultural round and poverty was just around the corner for all. The Lord of the Manor still exercised some of his medieval rights and the church still held a prominent position in the community. The parish officials appear to have been both conscientious and humane in carrying out their many duties.

There were advantages and disadvantages for the village being so close to London. Prosperous people retired to Eltham and benefited the community by their wider interests and the occasional charity endowed. Poorer people "landed on the doorstep" due to the two main roads through the town and had to be provided for by the parish. The prosperous benefitted from the healthier environment and could still keep up their London connections. The poor were looked after by the parish, particularly after the workhouse was built. The turnpiking of the main roads made life easier in many ways - produce from local farms could easily be taken to the London markets,and apprenticeships for local people were easier to obtain in the City.

As the century progressed Eltham was becoming more and more economically dependent on London; an omen for the future when the village was swallowed by the Metropolis.

Milestone, High Street outside
Chequers Public House

Amusements

TO TAKE PLACE AT THE ELTHAM

JUBILEE

5th. SEPTEMBER, 1833.

GINGLING MATCH,

All Persons to be properly attired.   No. 2,

Scrambling for Penny Pieces

Candidates not allowed to fall down.   No. 3,

Flogging the Ball out of the Hole,

No unfair whipping, and not to cut his neighbour too close.

EATING ROLLS & TREACLE

Boys to come with clean faces.   No. 5,

DIPPING FOR MARBLES,

No candidate to wear Hair Powder.   No. 6,

Dipping for Oranges,

No Boys to wear Night Caps, and their Mouths not to exceed
Six Inches.   No. 7,

Climbing the Pole,

No candidate to come with Bird Lime, no objection to Chaff.

No. 8,

JUMPING in SACKS

No Person will be admitted with a Wooden Leg.   No. 9,

HURDLE STAKES

Short Sighted Persons need not apply.   No. 10,

Carter's best *Mather Wool*, and best Crack of the Whip.

No Dumb Person to offer himself candidate.

UNDER THE MANAGEMENT OF

The Sub-committee, Messrs SMITH, LEKEUX, & ROBERT.

THE WHOLE TO CONCLUDE WITH

A Grand Display of Fire Works.

Notice of Shaw-Brooke Jubilee, 1833

56

IN THE YEAR OF THE GREAT EXHIBITION

Let us imagine ourselves being transported back in time to 1851, the year of the Great Exhibition at Hyde Park. Having arrived in Eltham from London let us call at the Vicarage and ask the Rev. Charles Gulliver Fryer, (aged 44 and born in Dorset) to leave his wife and their four servants at home for an afternoon and to show us around the parish in which he has ministered for a decade. He tells us that about a quarter of Eltham's people lived in the High Street area and the rest in hamlets or farms scattered around the parish. He also says that only about 350 of his parishioners worked directly on the land and the parish population had grown from 1,702 at the time of the first Census in 1801 to 2,578 today.

Vicar Fryer might show us the portrait of his influential predecessor, the Rev. J.K. Shaw-Brooke who held office during the period 1783-1840. This worthy gentleman had indexed the parish registers and taken a great interest in Eltham, its children and its poor. Rev. C. Fryer might speak of how older residents were always telling him of the virtues of his predecessor and reminiscing about the enormous Jubilee party that was celebrated in the Courtyard on September 5th 1833 to honour J.K. Shaw-Brooke's 50 years as Vicar of Eltham. In that year too, wooden weatherboarded houses named Jubilee Cottages had been erected just off the High Street where the rear of Allders store is now (145 High Street). A portrait of Rev. John Kenward Shaw-Brooke had been painted by John Hayes and paid for by public subscription.

Rev. J. K. Shaw-Brooke in old age, from his portrait S.F.C.

Rev. Charles Fryer would show us, his visitors, around the church. He would be conscious that the guidebook writer who termed it "a mean fabric, much patched and modernised with scarce a trace of anything like good work" (Churches of Kent, S. Glyne, 1830) was more accurate than malicious. He would know that the building could scarcely be adequate should the population of the parish continue to grow. The interior already had galleries dating from 1751 and 1764 as well as more elegant ones on delicate ironwork supports erected in 1819 and 1828. There was a Royal Coat of Arms dating from 1816 on the front of one of the galleries. He might speak of the non-conformists who worshipped in premises elsewhere in the town.

One of the galleries had been added specifically to accommodate the children of the National School. This had been established in 1813, largely through the influence of Rev. Shaw-Brooke. Vicar Fryer might take us to visit the school building situated in Pound Place. If the school was in session we would be introduced to Charles Sharpe, the 47 year-old schoolmaster and the three women who were also teachers. The first was Margaret Miller, a 37 year-old widow with two children to support. The second, Harriet Blackney was the 24 year-old wife of the local whitesmith. The third teacher was Ruth Pike, the 63 year-old widow of clockmaker, James Pike. She had also served Eltham as its postmistress during the years when postage stamps were first introduced. The schoolmaster could have spared time from his teaching to show us the admission register listing the first pupils in 1813. They were children of tradesmen, farmers, labourers and servants. Their average age on admission was eight years. The parents of some paid a small fee, but many were admitted free on the recommendation of one of the twelve managers. Since the schoolmaster's salary of £20 per annum was paid from the Leggatt Charity of 1714 its Trustees were therefore entitled to admit pupils. Many pupils in the school's early years left for apprenticeships or labouring work at the age of 10 or 11, their income desperately needed to support their families.

If we enquired about the future job prospects of Mr. Sharpe's present pupils in 1851 we might be told that they would be likely to follow in their parents and elder siblings footsteps into the building trade, shopkeeping, transport and services like hair cutting and chimney sweeping. Many would find domestic employment in the households of richer parishioners as cooks, maids, or garden staff. Some, from as young as 12 would be employed with 25 others in the envelope factory run by Mr. Gathercole of nearby Elm Terrace. James Gathercole, at 39 was one of the largest employers of labour in the district. He preferred to employ young women with nimble fingers. He had nine children at home but only one domestic servant.

Should we dare to query the health and safety of the working conditions among the paper and glue of Gathercole's Manufactory the Rev. Fryer might take us to meet Mr. Saunders, resident at Eltham Court, adjoining the Palace. Mr. Saunders had been appointed one of Her Majesty's first four Factory Inspectors on 1st October 1833. Initially, he was supposed to inspect 300 mills employing 24,000 people and later, 1193 mills from Yorkshire to the South East Coast became his responsibility. He had served on the Royal Commission on Children's Employment in 1841. Conditions at Gathercole's compared very favourably with some of the horrors in his reports.

If we, as visitors, then showed a particular interest in the fate of Eltham's great medieval hall, which was then serving as a barn. Rev. Fryer would have walked with us down Eltham Hill to Dr. David King's house, "King's Dene," at the corner of what is now Sherard Road, where he lived with John Morgan, his 25 year old assistant surgeon from Glamorganshire. Other members of his household were Henry Middleton, an invalid soldier, Mary White, his cook, Mary Lock, his housemaid, Fred Whittle, his groom and Charles Goulding, a keeper. Dr. King's hobby was the history of Eltham. On his bookshelf we might have seen an excellent volume on Eltham Palace produced by Dunnage and Laver in 1828. Dr. King spoke with pride of the work of the painters, Sandby and Turner, who had portrayed the ruined Great Hall at the beginning of the century and of the detailed architectural drawings J.C. Buckler had made between 1811 and 1828. He also spoke of his own exploration, together with architect A.B. Clayton, of the tunnels or cellars beneath the Palace site in the spring of 1834. In more recent years he had attempted to collect such documents as would clarify the history of the patronage of Eltham Vicarage.

Plaque commemorating the labourers who, in 1834, cleared the silted up sewers of the Palace

E.S.C.

Should we, the visitors, be foolish enough to comment that Eltham must be a remarkably healthy place, if its doctor has time to indulge in such antiquarian and archaeological hobbies, Dr. King might then reveal the caring and professional part of his personality. He might show us his notes on Sun Yard, where, behind the Rising Sun public house, people shared one communal water pump, sanitation was minimal and disease rife. He might walk us across to Kirk's Alley and Yard, near the White Hart where a similar situation could be found. Families with incomes of about 12 or 14 shillings for everyone's work, rents of about three shillings for their decrepit houses which shared a water supply with at least 13 other households, and frequent illnesses could scarcely afford the doctor's usual fee. Dr. King often treated them for little or nothing and charged higher fees to his more wealthy patients, such as the Lewins at Merlewood House and Barn House, the Gossetts at Eltham House or George Woolaston's family at Conduit House, to compensate for his own loss of income. Prescriptions given by Dr. David King were made up by Charles Mellin in his chemist's shop near the "Greyhound," now 90 High Street.

Mellins the Chemist and the Greyhound Inn
c. 1906   E.S.C.

With older members of the poor families, which Dr. King could have introduced us to, the conversation would lead back again to the good works of Rev. Shaw-Brooke. (Fryer would have felt, yet again, that he was a hard act to follow!) Shaw-Brooke had led the Parish opposition to the Board of Ordnance so that the poor of Eltham could continue taking loam, brushwood and clay from their own Common rather than having it monopolised by the military from Woolwich. He had organised the "Soup Society" which supplied a total of over 30,000 gallons of hot, cheap nourishment that sustained the poor in the 13 exceptionally hard winters that occurred between 1816-1847. The most enterprising of Eltham's poor in the mid-19th century adopted a drastic solution. They emigrated to Australia and New Zealand.

King George's Field, Eltham Common, 1990 showing Brook Hospital in background   *S.F.C.*

To save the time involved in visiting each of Eltham's farms, Rev. Fryer might, on returning to the church have produced the parish copy of The Tithe Plan, a colourful map about 6 feet square, detailing land use, ownership and occupiers in 1839. If we could avoid the then contentious issue of Commutation of Tithe and turn the conversation to people and agriculture we would soon learn that Mr. John Green of Southend was Eltham's major farmer, supervising a total of 1620 acres and employing 45 labourers. Thomas Blanchett, senior, was farm bailiff at Southend and Thomas Blanchett, junior, did the same job at Coldharbour. At Middle Park, Clay Farm and Eltham Park the chief householder was not a farmer, but the farmer or a farm bailiff lived nearby. For example, Henry William Dobell, Clerk in Her Majesty's Customs lived at Middle Park House with Thomas and Maria Wallis farming 120 acres and employing five labourers from their base at the nearby cottage. Thomas Jackson, an engineering contractor, was at the "Big House," while the Eltham Park's agriculture was supervised by Thomas Wakeham, whose wife Mary, was busy caring for their six children. At Chapel Farm, Horace and Ann Hammond farmed 248 acres with their 17 labourers. James and Mary Butler, with their three daughters, farmed the 211 acres at Horn Park, employing 12 labourers. At Mottingham, William Purvis, a Scotsman, farmed 132 acres, employing seven labourers. James Hill and James Marnham were farm bailiffs at Well Hall. The smallest acreage of any one farm was the 30 acres which Mary Ann Hooker, and her one employee, tilled at Pope Street. There were also market gardeners and cow keepers such as the two Joseph Ceelys, senior and junior, who worked in the area near the old Palace.

In 1839 Eltham's 3,713 cultivated acres had over 1,350 acres of meadow and pasture, over 1,400 acres of arable and many acres of woodland. Eltham Common had a further 42 acres and there were spacious gardens, orchards, private parkland, yards, ponds, roads and dwellings. Rev. Fryer suggested, as he rolled up the Tithe Map and put it into its box, that the situation was little changed in 1851.

As we prepared to take our leave of Rev. Fryer and his parishioners, he might have wondered when the railway would reach his parish of Eltham, and what changes it would bring to the community. To return to the Metropolis we could mount Mr. Stephen Scudd's horse omnibus or hire one of his private "flies" to the nearest railway stations at Blackheath or Woolwich. Blackheath Station had opened on 30th July 1849 and Woolwich Arsenal on 1st November that same year.

As we travel back to our own era we may list those 19th century buildings in Eltham which predate the coming of our first railway line in 1866....... numbers 7-16 Elizabeth Terrace; numbers 4, 23 and 24 Philipot Path; "Holbrook" (162)on Shooters Hill; Theobalds Cottages, 62-74 Avery Hill Road; Southwood House and Cottages (201-209), also in Avery Hill Road; St. Mary's Convent which is now the Community Centre at 180 Eltham High Street; Madras Villas, 2-14 Southend Crescent; 131a Eltham High Street; and "The Grange," at 468-472 Footscray Road.

The visitor today to the Parish Church of St. John's may see the memorial stone erected in memory of Dr. David King. This was financed by public subscription from grateful patients. The inscription on it notes that he died, aged 78, in 1865, after a residence of 54 years in the parish. Perhaps to some of the inhabitants of the parish in 1851 we owe the naming of two Elthams in Australia (Victoria, 1873, and New South Wales, settled 1860 but finally named in 1894) and Eltham (New Zealand, 1884).

Theobalds Cottages, Avery Hill Road, photographed 1990

S.F.C.

ELTHAM IN 1839

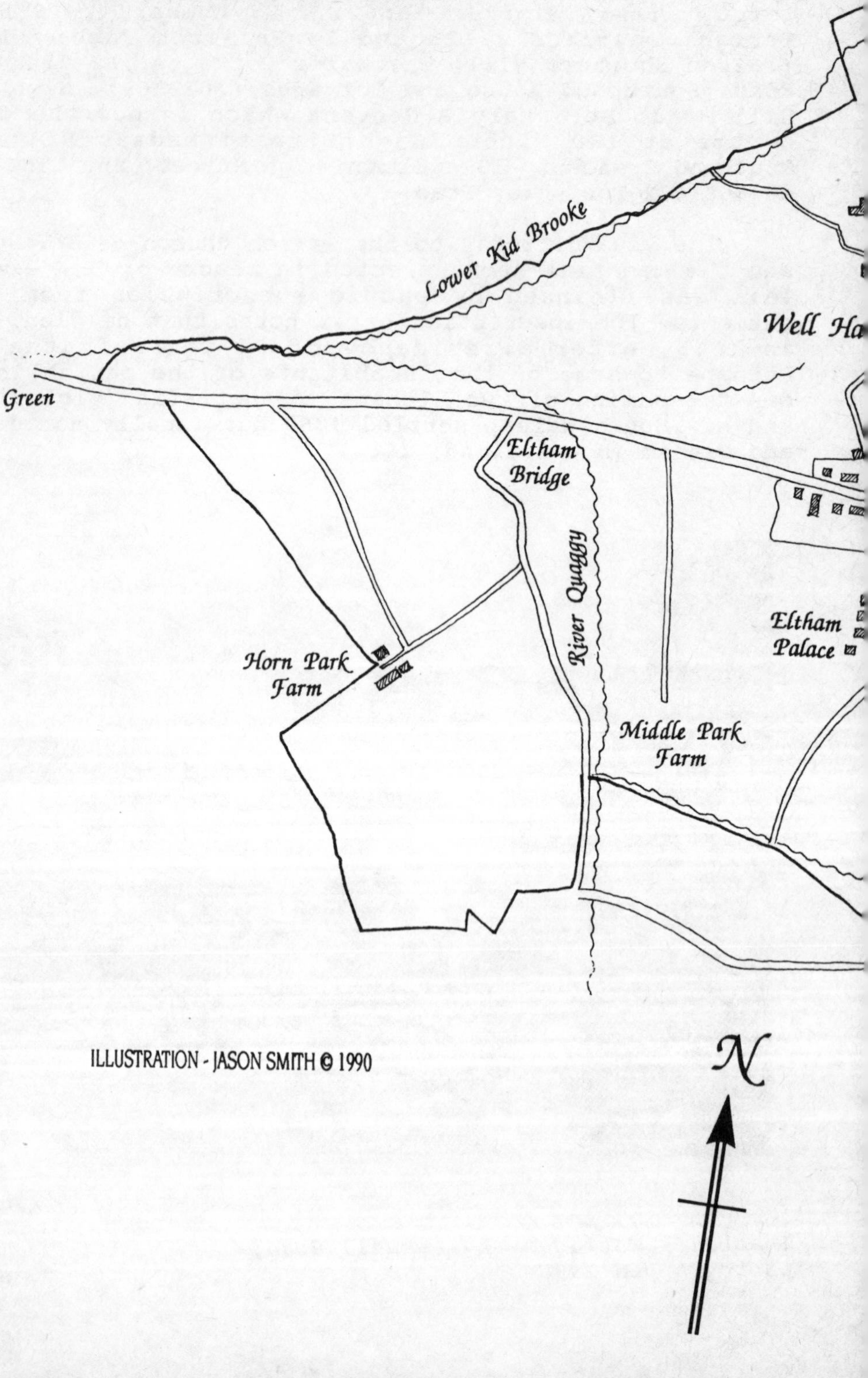

Lower Kid Brooke

Well Ha

Lee Green

Eltham
Bridge

River Quaggy

Horn Park
Farm

Eltham
Palace

Middle Park
Farm

ILLUSTRATION - JASON SMITH © 1990

N

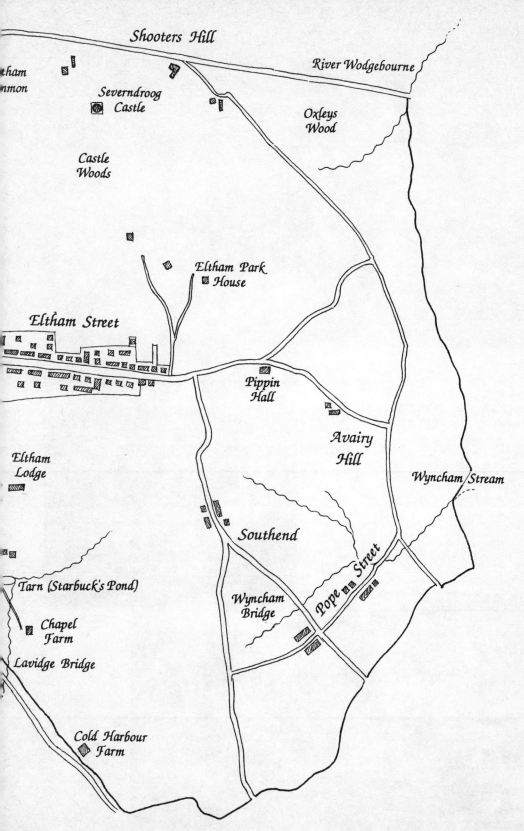

Shooters Hill

River Wodgebourne

Severndroog
Castle

...tham
...mmon

Oxleys
Wood

Castle
Woods

Eltham Park
House

Eltham Street

Pippin
Hall

Avairy
Hill

Wyncham Stream

Eltham
Lodge

Southend

Tarn (Starbuck's Pond)

Wyncham
Bridge

Pope Street

Chapel
Farm

Lavidge Bridge

Cold Harbour
Farm

*Some of the villas built
in Eltham for Victorian
commuters photographed 1990*

S.F.C.

THE AGE OF STEAM

The first Eltham Station (now Mottingham) was opened on 1st September 1866 at a spot in the middle of fields with no habitation to the south until Mottingham village was reached and little to the north except the ruins of Eltham Palace and the village of Eltham. The former cart track of Chapel Farm Lane with its bends was transformed into the present Court Road and spoil from the railway cuttings had raised its level at Starbuck's Pond (now The Tarn) to take the road by bridge over the new railway. Some years later the road was laid through into Mottingham.

A steam train arrives at Mottingham Station, early 20th century   G.W.C.

Most of the land south of the High Street, Eltham, was owned by the Crown and the attractions of housing development were soon to be seen along Court Road, North Park (only at the east end), Wellington Road (now Wythfield Road), Victoria Road (now Footscray Road) and later at West Park, formerly West Chislehurst Park at Mottingham. The properties were mostly large detached villas to lure wealthy city magnates to Eltham's country aspects and each residence would need its army of servants to keep the properties in the condition that was demanded by the Crown leases. Carriages would take the new Eltham residents to Eltham Station where steam trains would speed them to their city offices, although during the day there were only eleven stopping trains in each direction. Cobblestones of the horse stand can still be seen outside the station on the down side roadway.

The new wealth attracted to Eltham manifested itself in the construction of new churches :- Eltham Congregational Church (1868), Holy Trinity (1869), St. Peter's, Lee (1871), St. Andrew's (1879) and St. Mary's R.C. (1890). The much repaired old church of St. John the Baptist was rebuilt in 1875 to the design of the architect, Arthur Blomfield. It is still a major landmark in central Eltham. A new Eltham National School was built at the end of Roper Street in 1868 to replace that in Pound Place. This would serve a growing child population of less wealthy residents and be in readiness to operate the 1870 Education Act with its target of compulsory schooling for all - at a price. The houses in Roper Street were completed soon after the school was opened.

Eltham Church of England Primary School,
Roper Street, 1990   S.F.C.

The station at Pope Street (now New Eltham) spawned the development of large detached villas in what we now know as Southwood Road, Avery Hill Road and Footscray Road as well as the terraced cottages for the less wealthy in roads like Novar, Gaitskell, Reventlow, Lannoy, Merchland and Batturs (Blanmerle). Developments in this area were a little later as the station did not open until 1878. The All Saints, Pope Street Mission Church started in a hut by the railway where the Telecom vehicles are now parked in Avery Hill Road whilst a permanent church at Bercta Road was erected. This opened in 1898 with a nave and tin chancel only. The infant building at the Pope Street School (Wyborne) was opened in 1881 as one of the new Board Schools which were not under church jurisdiction as was the case with the National Schools.

The development of these new areas was greatly aided by the construction of the West Kent Sewer which was constructed under a statute of 1875. However, by 1882 Pope Street and New Eltham were still not connected and a petition was presented by the Plumstead Board of Works insisting that this work be carried out to take the new houses away from cesspit drainage which presented difficulties due to the clay nature of the soil.

Fresh water was provided by the Kent Water Works Board and replaced, or aided the standpipes which were a necessity for some homes - an externally restored standpipe can be seen in the grounds of the Fifteen Penny Fields Almshouses in Blunts Road. This originally stood by the High Street, opposite the Fire Station. K.W.W. hydrant covers are evident on pavements in roads laid down in Victorian times. The first Eltham Reservoir was built in the High Street in 1890/1 behind Montrose House and has a capacity of three million gallons. Improvements in health were an important aspect of Victorian philosophy especially as the London cholera epidemic of 1834 had caused great loss of life.

Kent Water Works hydrant cover in Southwood Road, New Eltham, 1990   *S.F.C.*

A local cottage hospital started in 1880 in a house which became part of Hitches Garage (43 High Street, adjacent to Sowerby Close) when larger premises were opened in 1898 at Passey Place. Even so, many of the poorer cottages around the High Street were the subject of a report of 1896 which condemned the "insanitary condition of Eltham." In 1901 the Medical Officer of Health for the London County Council (L.C.C.) made reference to Sun Yard, Kirk's Yard and Scriven Alley where the cottages were built back to back with other buildings.

"The height of rooms in Sun Yard varied from 6'6" to 5'7" and the cubic contents from 983 cu.ft. to 576 cu.ft.; the houses are without floor ventilation and protection from ground effluvia and the joists appear to rest on the floor."

There were few improvements in road transport compared with the railways and Eltham was very reliant on the horse for moving heavy loads. People who could afford the fare rode in carts and carriages. In 1854 Scudd's Railway Omnibus was advertised as running between The Castle, Eltham, to London by way of Lee and Blackheath (North Kent Railway). In the 1860's Thomas Tillings took over the route and were running horse buses between Eltham and Blackheath as late as 1908.

Eltham High Street c. 1905 showing Tillings horse-drawn bus

E.S.C.

Horse troughs were bought through the Metropolitan Drinking and Cattle Trough Association with the help of local pressure and finance and examples can still be seen at Eltham Green Road and Clare Corner, Green Lane. Sign posts were positioned to help the occasional traveller including the cyclist and examples of such posts can be seen at Clare Corner and at the junction of Avery Hill Road and Halfway Street in the form of finger posts.

Horse trough and finger post, Clare Corner,
New Eltham, 1990   *S.F.C.*

The Cyclists Touring Club Companion to the British Road Book, 1898 states:

"From Lee Green....we approach gradually towards the country along a road so disgracefully "bumpy" that breakages of springs and other small parts of machines are common among local cyclists. This remark applies also to the road between Eltham and Sidcup which is shamefully neglected in spite of the heavy traffic along it all the year round. Eltham, the main street, is narrow and usually very muddy."

Until 1868 travellers to London had to pay a toll to use the roads that were administered by the New Cross Turnpike Trust and the first tollgate out of Eltham was at Lee near the present Cambridge Road junction. A small cottage housed the toll-keeper and his family and the last occupier of this position was Mr. William Crawley. His family came from a long line of toll-keepers, his mother looked after the gate at Crook Log, Bexleyheath. Royalty used to go through the Lee Gate to the Eltham Races. The Prince of Wales, later King Edward VII, the Duke of Edinburgh and other members of the Royal Family drove down from London in a coach with postillions. Race day was the busiest of the year and takings were from £25-£30 in sums of 3d., 6d. and a shilling. The days of the stage coaches to Maidstone, Dover and Folkestone were over, for the railways were able to provide a quicker service to and from London with no stopping to change horses. Relics of the New Cross Turnpike Trust and the horse drawn coaching era can be seen in the form of milestones on the road through Eltham and New Eltham to Footscray.

As there was no permanent fire station in Eltham, a fire escape, stand and watch box were kept on a piece of land in Blunts Road where the L.C.C. paid a rent of five shillings to the Eltham Charity (1891). In 1881 Pope Street residents were provided with a 600 feet long hose and reel to be stored in a shed next to the Beehive Public House. A year later they were granted two portable fire ladders and two light trucks mounted on wheels each to carry six lengths of ordinary scaling ladders.

In 1839 Eltham became and still is, part of "R" Division of the Metropolitan Police. The 1851 census states that five P.C's. and their families lived in police cottages at the corner of Pound Place and the High Street (202 High Street) but larger premises were available in 1865 when the new station was opened at the corner of the present Footscray Road and the High Street.

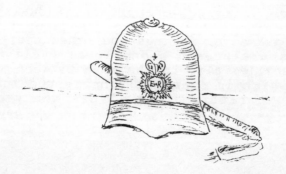

The brewing of beer was an occupation practised in many larger Kentish villages like Eltham and distinctive buildings for this purpose were erected on the site of the former St. John's vicarage, next to Sowerby Close, in 1872. The buildings included a tun room, washing and bottling room, ice house, fermenting room, boiler, stables, harness room, manager's house and a cottage. The architect was Arthur Kinder. Several of Eltham's pubs were built in Victorian times or rebuilt to a larger design. The surviving examples are The Park Tavern, The Man of Kent (1888) and The Beehive (1897).

The Beehive Public House, New Eltham, 1990   *S.F.C.*

The increase in size of St. John's cemetery indicates a larger population by the number of burials. Local dignitaries like Colonel North (1842-1896), the "Nitrate King" of Avery Hill and William Blenkiron (1809-1871), horse breeder of Middle Park Farm, were buried here with large monuments to match their earthly status. In an unmarked grave lie the remains of Richard Oliver Launcelot Jefferies who died in 1885 of meningitis at under two years of age. He lived with his parents at what is now 59 Footscray Road where a Greater London Council(G.L.C.) blue plaque records the residence of his father, the author Richard Jefferies. In 1868, at 3 Wythfield Road (then Wellington Road) was born Edward Verrall Lucas. His family were Quakers and they moved to Brighton where he received his education. As E.V. Lucas he wrote many books including anthologies and travel guides and was an authority on the author, Charles Lamb.

Mr. Benjamin Wood, a hop merchant and M.P. for the "Borough" (Southwark) moved into Eltham Lodge in 1838 with his wife, Anna. He died in 1845 but she survived him until her death in 1889 aged 98. In 1875 she bought one of the new detached houses in North Park called Wonersh Lodge (Woodington Close site) for her niece, Kitty O'Shea and her husband so that she could be a companion to her Aunt "Ben." Kitty's subsequent friendship with Charles Stewart Parnell, leader of the party advocating Irish Home Rule, led to her unsavoury divorce, their short marriage and removal to Brighton. Parnell died in 1891. Eltham Lodge and grounds were leased by the Crown to the Eltham Golf Club in 1892 and this arrangement continued until they amalgamated with the Royal Blackheath Golf Club after the First World War.

In 1889 Eltham's link with Kent, to which she had been attached since recorded time, was severed when union with the new County Of London was forged by an Act of Parliament.

The name of "Kent" lingered on in the postal address but the mould had been set. The opening of the Bexleyheath Railway to the north of Eltham's village centre in 1895 heralded greater development. This seemed to be hastened when Eltham became part of the new Woolwich Borough Council in 1900 at a time when relief came to Mafeking if not to Eltham's village status.

High Street c. 1880 looking towards the Greyhound, via the Philip Lane Collection

Queen Victoria died in 1901 which brought her long reign to an end in a period where tremendous expansion had taken place in the empire and at home. The effect on Eltham was marginal in comparison but the seeds were sown for greater growth in the twentieth century.

THE RISE OF SUBURBIA

A little before midnight on 31st December 1900 the muffled bells of St. John's Parish Church, Eltham tolled the passing of the year. Then, they pealed out their welcome to the new year 1901, accompanied by the distant sound of the ships in London's docks, welcoming the new year with hooters and sirens. Twenty two days later the townsfolk of Eltham would join with Britons everywhere in mourning the death of Queen Victoria. All those of age 60 and under would have known no other monarch, but they would shortly be celebrating the coronation of King Edward VII.

Without radio or television the residents of Eltham would have learned of these momentous events from the newspapers bought possibly from Franklin's newsagent's opposite the parish church. Stood in his shop, Mr. Franklin would have noticed many times the cows from Lyme Farm, being taken via Wellington Road (now Wythfield Road) to the meadows behind Eltham Palace. Lyme Farm was later to become the site of the Borough Council's Page Estate.

The meadows near Eltham Palace, c. 1973   J.K.C.

In those early days of the new King's reign, before Well Hall Road had been widened and extended to the High Street, between the parish and Congregational churches, any townsfolk wishing to visit Woolwich would have walked or taken the horse bus. It infrequently ran from Tilling's Yard, next to "The Greyhound" public house via Sherard Gardens (now Sherard Road) which passed Well Hall Railway Station, opened in 1895. Some also rode on the horse bus to Colonel North's Avery Hill estate and enjoyed a walk through the grounds on spring and summer afternoons. On a sunny Sunday evening they would have enjoyed the band which was given permission to play there. Colonel North's Avery Hill estate was purchased by the London County Council in 1902, who opened it as a public park the following year.

The Winter Gardens at Avery Hill, c. 1972   *E.S.C.*

At the beginning of King Edward VII's reign Eltham was a country village. Farms, woodlands and open spaces including meadows surrounded it on all sides. Lyme Farmhouse stood on Eltham Hill, a little to the west of the junction with Sherard Road. The Middle Park Estate now covers part of Middle Park Farm, which was managed by Farmer Bailey. A meandering river Quaggy ran through its fields. Coldharbour Farm was situated in the area of the present Coldharbour Estate.

Pippen Hall Farm of Mr. Grace. lay on the southern side of Bexley Road, near the present Oakways Estate. Mr. Edward Sheppard's Well Hall Farm lay to the west of Well Hall Road, in the vicinity of Arbroath Road. The Shooters Hill woodlands reached as far as what is now the Bexley Road in the area known as Crown Woods.

An Edwardian view of Chapel Farm,
Mottingham   *E.S.C.*

On 1st May 1895 the Bexley Heath Railway Company had opened the Bexleyheath Line with a local station at Well Hall. The coming of this railway, together with the Loop Line running through New Eltham and Mottingham, was the main impetus towards new house building and suburbanisation of the district.

In 1899 340 acres of land had become available at Eltham Park, very close to the centre of village Eltham, and was soon bought by the Scottish Liberal M.P., Mr. A. Cameron Corbett. He also carried out speculative building at Ilford and Hither Green. Between 1900 and 1914 the first of Eltham's housing estates was built on this land. The houses, all sturdily built and spaciously placed, varied from small, terraced properties to large, double-fronted, detached villas. The straight roads were laid out in a gridiron pattern, and most were given Scottish names by Corbett himself.

Corbett houses at Eltham Park Gardens, c. 1969 via Alan A. Jackson Collection

A year after the King's death Cameron Corbett was created Baron Rowallan. He was a strong advocate of temperance, and refused to allow any public houses or off licences on the estate. He realised that a good railway connection to the City of London was vital to the success of the development, and offered financial support to the South Eastern and Chatham Railway to get them to build a station in a strategic position. He requested "superior passenger accommodation" and the station, opened on 1st July 1908 as "Shooters Hill," had covered access ramps and long canopies on both platforms. It was later renamed "Eltham Park." Churches for four different denominations were built; St. Luke's Church of England (1907), Baptist (1903), Methodist (1902, present building 1906) and Eltham Park Independent Chapel (1913). Two schools were opened on the estate; Grangehill Road (later renamed "The Gordon School") in February 1902 and Deansfield Road in

On the edge of the new estate in Well Hall Road, close to the "Well Hall" Station a parade of shops was built, and in St. Luke's Church Magazines for 1905 advertisements indicate the variety of shops recently opened. In addition to a dairy, a butcher, a baker and greengrocer, was a watchmaker and jeweller, a dressmaker and costumier and a chemist and optician. In 1906 the Royal Arsenal Co-operative Society store at Well Hall was built. These, together with the shops in the High Street saw that new arrivals on the estate were well catered for.

In 1905 Well Hall Road from the railway bridge at Well Hall to Eltham parish church was completed. During its building Walter Colston Brake, a builder, leased land from the Polhill family and on the western side of the new road built what is now called "The Old Page Estate." It comprised four roads; Spencer Gardens, Sherard Gardens (now Sherard Road), Everest Road and Lassa Road, and was built between 1906 and 1912, Spencer Gardens being the first, and Lassa Road the last.

Well Hall Road - Spencer Gardens, c. 1906   *J.K.C.*

Perhaps the most important single building to be created in King Edward's reign was Eltham Library. Shortly after Eltham became part of the Metropolitan Borough of Woolwich in 1900, the Public Libraries Acts were adopted for the Borough, and Dr. Andrew Carnegie gave £14,000 towards the building of libraries at Plumstead and Eltham. Dr. Carnegie was a Scottish born American philanthropist who gave money for the building of libraries in the United States of America and Great Britain. Mr. Maurice B. Adams F.R.I.B.A., the architect, was approached to design and plan the Eltham Library. It was built by the Council's direct labour department under the supervision of the Borough Engineer, Mr. J. Rush Dixon M.I.C.E. and the Eltham Buildings Committee. It remains to this day a fine piece of Edwardian architecture. The Library, opened on Tuesday 23rd October 1906 by the Mayor, Dr. Gilbert Slater J.P., stood on a portion of a site acquired by the Council for the purpose of erecting a public hall, district offices and public baths. So says the "Programme of Proceedings" at the official opening, but the rest of the site was never used for these buildings.

Eltham Library, High Street, 1989   *S.F.C.*

Other premises built during King Edward's reign included The Chequers Public House (1903), The Rising Sun Public House (1904), both unaltered and still flourishing in 1989. The Eltham Fire Station was opened in 1904 and the fire engines from this building have served the townsfolk of Eltham ever since.

The Rising Sun Public House, High Street, 1989   S.F.C.

Throughout these years repairs were carried out to the Great Hall of Eltham Palace. Captain and Mrs. Wilson lived in the house which stood in the moated area immediately across the bridge, and on the then earthen floor of the Great Hall, they had a tennis court.

On 6th May 1910 King Edward died at Buckingham Palace. To the people of Eltham and elsewhere, this news, read in the newspapers the following day, would have come as a sudden shock. It had not been realised that the King had been so ill.

During this year of 1910 the tramway from Woolwich to Eltham via the new Well Hall Road, had been laid. It was built after repeated requests by the residents of Eltham and Well Hall, especially from those living on the new Corbett Estate who had found work in Woolwich. The service began on 23rd July 1910, with new trams costing £950 each.

Despite the building of the Corbett and Brake Estates the area around the centre of Eltham at this time was still mainly rural. There were not only dairy farms, wheat and barley was grown extensively. Wheat fields flourished where the Westhorne Avenue now runs through the centre of the Page Estate.

The citizens of Eltham, as in the rest of the country, had now settled contentedly under the new monarch, King George V. They did not know that in four years time the young men of the country would be remorselessly drawn into the most terrible conflict that fighting men would ever have to endure.

In the meantime many worked hard on the farms and in the shops for very low wages. Some found it difficult to make ends meet, and were to be seen on Mondays taking clothes and goods to the pawnbroker in Lee to receive a few shillings that would help them through the week. They would walk to Lee again on Saturdays to retrieve what they had left.

George Edward French, Sadlers & Harness Makers c. 1902. 158 High Street now stands there. via the Bert French Collection

Life was hard for the lower classes in those days. When they had money they shopped, as now, mainly within the confines of the High Street. Their clothes, curtains, buttons and blinds would have been obtained from the drapers, Narbeth's, later George's of 92-94 High Street. W.F. Lowater was Eltham's nurseryman, seedsman and florist at No.3 Courtyard with the nursery off Park Place (now Passey Place). Through the doors of Cave Austin and Co. Ltd., grocers at 96-98 High Street would come the very pleasant smell of coffee beans being ground. Tools, nails and hardware would have been bought at Grummitt's Stores in Courtyard.

The First World War started on 4th August 1914 and as in the rest of the country, it was to draw many of Eltham's young men to the terrifying trench warfare across the English Channel. The names of those who did not return are set out on the War Memorial situated in the St.John's churchyard wall in the High Street. Starting with A.E. Adams and ending with H. Young, 276 names are listed. The manufacture of munitions became a top priority and many workers were required at the Woolwich Arsenal. So many were needed that it became necessary for the authorities to provide homes within easy reach of their place of work, and the southern slopes of Shooters Hill were deemed suitable for housing development. So another part of village Eltham gradually disappeared when 96 acres of farmland astride the Well Hall Road were taken up by the Well Hall Garden City, now the Progress Estate. The entire estate was built between February and December 1915. It was considered to be a fantastic achievement of so called "cottage housing," and credit should go to the architect, Sir Frank Baines, who controlled the project. It is said that no two houses are alike. The estate is now designated a Conservation Area.

Early Days at Admiral Seymour Road,
Progress Estate,   *E.S.C.*

As the war progressed more and yet more workers of all categories were required in the factories of the Royal Arsenal at Woolwich. It was estimated that an additional 20,000 would be required in the new workshops that were to be opened. All the houses on the new Progress Estate were soon taken and it became obvious that many more dwellings would be needed.

The matter was resolved by the construction of temporary wooden units and hostels. Construction of the Eltham Hutments started in October 1915 in the area now known as the "Castlewood Estate." These so called "temporary bungalows" were also built on Mr. Edward Sheppard's farmland at Well Hall, with the largest concentration on the Corbett Estate where the war had put a stop to building works. They provided reasonably comfortable family homes for about 20 years.

The "Hutments" at Arbroath Road and the first
St. Barnabas Church, C. 1917,
via the K. Blake Collection

Living in Eltham during the first twenty years of this century were some notable personalities; some famous and some more locally well known. Perhaps the most important figure as far as Eltham was concerned was Richard Robert Castell Gregory. He was headmaster of Eltham National Schools from 1901-1920 and was considered to be one of the "handful of gifted and dedicated amateurs" who turned England into a literate nation. On 8th October 1901 he found, in the depths of a cupboard, the Admission Register for the school in 1814. This formed the inspiration of his teaching of local history. Attendance at a Royal Garden Party gave official recognition to his wide service to education. He published "The Story of Royal Eltham" in 1909. It sold then for 5s Per copy and it is now a much treasured volume in the homes of Eltham residents. It lovingly tells of rural Eltham before its imminent smothering in suburbanisation, and is essential reading for all those who seek to learn about Eltham's illustrious past.

During 1899 there moved into the ancient, dilapidated, but dignified Well Hall, Mr. and Mrs. Hubert Bland and family. Mrs. Bland was the writer, E. Nesbit who became famous as the author of "The Story of the Treasure Seekers" (1899), "The Book of Dragons" (1900), "The Red House" (1903), "The Railway Children" (1906), and many other notable works. Although christened Edith, to her family, even into adult life, she was known as "Daisy." In order to amuse her own and other children she built "Magic Cities" by using a variety of lids, salt cellars, assorted containers and bric-a-brac. One was displayed at a charity exhibition at Olympia in 1912 where numerous readers were able to meet her. She was a notable figure in Eltham and would be seen, usually in a flowing cape, when the trams were running past Well Hall, taking a jug of tea out to the tram drivers. Hubert, her husband, died in April 1914, but she surprised all her friends when she re-married on 20th February 1917, "A soul of goodness and kindness," named Thomas Terry Tucker. She died on Sunday 4th May 1924 and she was buried in the churchyard of St. Mary in the Marsh, Kent, in accordance with her wishes.

Another famous person who resided locally was the cricketer, W.G. Grace. William Gilbert Grace was born on 18th July 1848 at Downend, near Bristol. He studied at Bristol and then at Westminster Hospital, after which he began to practise as a doctor in 1879. He spent the last year of his life at "Fairmount" in Mottingham Lane, which now has a Blue Plaque commemorating his life there. W.G. Grace played his last cricket match for Eltham Cricket Club against Grove Park on 25th July 1914, scoring 69 not out. He died in 1915 and was buried at Elmers End Cemetery.

On 5th February 1920 Dr. C. Addison, the then Minister of Health, cut the first sod near the top of Eltham Hill and started the building of the Woolwich Borough Council's Page Estate. Much house building subsequently followed until the country village which existed at the turn of the century became the pleasant suburb that exists today.

A20 Sidcup Road at the Crossways intersection,
1990   *S.F.C.*

Traffic moving along Westhorne Avenue towards
Well Hall Roundabout, 1990   *S.F.C.*

BETWEEN THE WARS

During the period 1920-1939 more physical change happened to Eltham than at any other time in its history. The transformation from farmland to suburb was almost completed while the creation of public parks and open spaces helped to preserve some of the rural areas for leisure purposes and green "lungs."

In hindsight, the period under consideration dealt with the recovery from one world war, a difficult financial situation throughout the world including going off the Gold Standard, and preparations for the next war. For many people the twenties were times of financial hardship and lack of permanent work. Servicemen who had returned to a supposed "land fit for heroes" found that their wartime patriotic duty was often sadly unrewarded.

Although the General Strike of May 1926 only lasted a week its problems rumbled on for some time and were symptomatic of the age. Times seemed to pick up in the mid 1930's with patriotic fervour expressing itself in the Silver Jubilee of King George V and Queen Mary in 1935. The death of the King in 1936 was followed some months later by the abdication of King Edward VIII. The succession of George VI and Queen Elizabeth and their Coronation in 1937 provided a time of popular acclaim which concealed the effect of Germany's massive re-armament which culminated in our entry into the Second World War.

The plight of the unemployed in the early 1920's prompted politicians, both locally and nationally to provide work of a useful nature. Pre-war plans for new roads to by-pass town and village centres were dusted down and amended where necessary and construction soon started using many men from the ranks of the unemployed. The Eltham By-Pass, now known as Sidcup Road, was opened in 1923 with financial help from the London County Council. It followed part of the original Mottingham Lane to the railway bridge and then ran over open countryside in its three mile length to Kemnal, Sidcup.

The draining of Harrow Meadows on either side of the meandering River Quaggy was a difficult task due to the nature of the soil and hand-propelled tip carts had to be used on the most difficult parts of the work which included taming the river into an open concrete culvert. On completion of the reclamation scheme new recreational facilities were provided and the whole area was opened in 1937 by the Mayor of Woolwich, Mabel Crout, with the name of Sutcliffe Park in memory of a former Borough Engineer. Other relief schemes for the unemployed included the South Circular Road (Westhorne Avenue), Shooters Hill By-Pass (Rochester way), Eltham Open Air Baths and the Avery Hill Road sewer.

The construction of the new roads allowed more houses to be built by the Woolwich Borough Council and private developers. In 1927 Charles and Daniel Barwell started their Belmont Park Estate at New Eltham which covered a pre-war golf course where roads like Montbelle, Felhampton and Larchwood now stand. Some houses were also built in Sidcup Road and these and later housing along this road created what became known as "ribbon development." This was outlawed on main roads

by an Act of the mid 1930's which accounts for the later construction of the service roads alongside the Sidcup Road near Mottingham Station. Private development on farmland included the Alanwood Estate on Clay Farm and the Davis Estate at Belmont Farm (Domonic Drive area) while woodland was cleared for houses in Avery Hill and Sidewood Roads and for the Eltham Heights Estate at Crown Woods.

Sewer renewal,
Avery Hill Road, c 1930

J.K.C.

Woolwich Borough Council constructed many houses in the Eltham area between the wars on former farmland. The Page Estate was started in 1920 and took ten years to complete. Stretching from Eltham Hill to the Progress Estate in one direction it covers land bought by Sir Gregory Page of Blackheath in 1733 from the Roper family. Until 1920 it formed part of Lyme Farm. Various styles of terrace and semi-detached houses can be perceived on a perambulation of the estate which reflects architectural and financial considerations. To rehouse the Eltham hutment tenants the Crown sold Middle Park and part of Horn Park Farms to the Council. The development included houses and flats and some very narrow roads which create problems for today's motorists.

Edgeworth Road on the Page Estate showing the problems of car parking in the narrow roads, 1990   *S.F.C.*

All new housing developments called for neighbourhood shopping centres, schools and particularly churches and this pattern was reflected in all new parts of Eltham.

It is interesting to note where all these new Eltham residents came from. The bulk of Council tenants were from the Woolwich and Plumstead areas seeking a home in the greener parts of the borough and in the case of Middle Park were mainly from the Eltham hutments. The private dwellings often housed people who were relocating from other parts of Eltham or were moving out, often as newly weds from inner London areas like Camberwell, New Cross and Lewisham but rarely from across the River Thames.

Mr. Lowater's delivery van   *E.S.C.*

Although horses were in use for local deliveries including bread and milk, the internal combustion engine was making use of the new roads while delivery by lorry and van increased considerably.

Measures to prevent road accidents were introduced including the provision of better street lighting. The first traffic lights in the Eltham area became operative on 30th January 1933 at the junction of Rochester way and Westmount Road and others quickly followed at Well Hall Road/Shooters Hill, Sidcup and Court Roads, High Street and Well Hall Road and Green Lane and Sidcup Road. Public telephone boxes were also appearing as were police telephone boxes, the first being installed near the Crossways Hotel by Sidcup Road in 1933.

To cater for the increasing numbers of private motorists petrol stations of a modest architectural style were constructed in the mid 1920's, which included the wooden Ace Garage at the northern junction of Sidcup Road and Green Lane. Very few original petrol stations or garages have survived into the 1990's but the garage which gave its name to a roundabout on the Sidcup Road - Clifton's (1936) is still intact (1989) though its connection with the Clifton family has long passed. The premises are no more than a petrol station while the post Second World war showroom and workshops on the other side of the roundabout are now used for other purposes.

Clifton's Garage, c. 1964   J.K.C.

Public transport became more popular and major improvement in services and facilities helped to satisfy this need. The tram lines from Lee were extended to Lyme Farm, by the junction with Eltham Hill and Sherard Road and the extension of route 46 to this terminus commenced on 29th November 1920. A further extension to join the existing terminus at Eltham Church was opened on 22nd March 1921 which necessitated the demolition of older property including The King's Arms public house to facilitate road widening. The completion of the railway bridge over Westhorne Avenue in 1932 enabled the road to be used by route 72 which ran from the Embankment (Savoy Street) to Woolwich.

Buses in Southend Crescent, 1929   *J.K.C.*

Bus services gradually increased in number so that by the time of the creation of London Transport on 1st July 1933 the main daily Eltham routes were:-

20	Turnpike Lane Station - Welling	
21	Wood Green - Farningham	
109	Penge - Welling	
132a	Lewisham - Bexley	
209	Forest Hill - Bexley	
422	Well Hall Station - Orpington	
610	Well Hall Station - Chislehurst (weekdays)	

By October 1938 the Eltham routes were:-

21	Turnpike Lane - Sidcup Garage
61	Well Hall Station - Orpington
124	Forest Hill - Eltham (Southend Crescent)
132	Lewisham - Bexley Station
132a	Well Hall Station - Bexleyheath
160	Catford - Welling
161	Chislehurst - Eltham (Southend Crescent)
228	Eltham - Chislehurst

Falconwood Station Ticket Hall, 1990   S.F.C.

   The biggest advance on the railways was the
electrification of the trains using the third rail system in
the mid 1920's. The line through New Eltham and Mottingham
was advertised to start on 12th July 1926; the work involved
on the Bexleyheath Line included a large, brick built,
electricity sub-station at Eltham Park Station. Increases in
traffic necessitated the rebuilding in brick of the Eltham
Well Hall Station in 1932 while extra bus passengers began to
arrive on 7th October 1931 when green single-decker route 422
arrived from Orpington and parked in Sherard Road and started
a trend which has made this area of Eltham the principle
terminus for Eltham bus routes. Further passengers used the
Bexleyheath Line after the new station was opened at
Falconwood at the beginning of 1936 which served the growing
estate built principally by New Ideal Homesteads.

Those people with an adventurous spirit could take to the air from a makeshift landing stage for aeroplanes at Harrow Meadows when the Cornwall Aviation Company hit the town. In April 1928 the Mayor, Councillor G.H. Langham and the Town Clerk, Sir Arthur Bryceson, took to the air for an aerial survey of parts of the Borough. For five shillings people queued for the chance to take to the air. This popular attraction also offered a chance to "loop the loop" for which the charge was fifteen shillings.

Boys of the Gordon School pose for the camera
with their Headmaster, Mr. Creese, in 1937   J.K.C.

The increase in the population from the new estates created a need for many new facilities. The London County Council designed schools of a different character to those to be seen at Deansfield, Gordon and Wyborne as solidness gave way to a cottage style of architecture at Haimo and Briset whereas Ealdham and Henwick reflect the three decker tradition with box-like classrooms but with a modern and generally airy situation. Schools generally had a leaving age of 14 years whilst selective education was available at Eltham Hill and the Woolwich Polytechnic where trade scholarships were offered.

With incredible foresight the Woolwich Borough Council, often in collaboration with the London County Council, ensured that the environmental mistakes that occurred in Woolwich and Plumstead were not repeated in the development of Eltham. The preservation of the southern slopes of Shooters Hill by a policy of direct acquisition when land became available excluded development of the type that was allowed on the northern slopes of the hill. New parks were created out of farmland and aged oaks and elms were retained in the parks and open spaces on the new estates. Queenscroft Recreational Ground's natural features helped to create a paddling pool which was graced by old trees from the days of Middle Park Farm. The presence of mature oak trees in Dunkery Road on the London County Council's estate at Mottingham give a connection with the long history of the former farmland.

Post World War II aerial view of Eltham Palace   *J.K.C.*

The purchase of the lease on Eltham Palace by Stephen Courtauld in 1933 from the Crown included many nearby fields and this enabled the ancient royal complex of buildings to secure a timeless setting which is often denied to some venerable buildings in suburban settings. Mr. Courtauld restored the Great Hall at considerable personal cost and built Eltham Hall as a family residence to the designs of Seeley and Paget. For some people with comments like "Romance dies at Eltham" the Hall was an unwelcome intrusion but time has allowed the two buildings of different ages to harmonise and mellow.

Other buildings of a distinctly 1930's flavour can be seen in the cinemas at Eltham Hill and Well Hall and the parade of shops at the corner of Sidcup and Southwood Roads at the Crossways. Architects Cachemaille-Day and Lander produced a church of unique design at St. Saviour's, Middle Park Avenue whose style is of continuing interest to students of architecture and is often featured in books of the period. As a contrast, St. Barnabas at Well Hall, which had started life as a wooden church on the corner of Arbroath Road was also consecrated in 1933. This is a Victorian church that was transported piece by piece from the Woolwich Dockyard where it was built to serve the Royal Marines and had subsequently become disused for church purposes.

The Coronet Cinema opened as the Odeon in 1936   *S.F.C.*

The United Reform Church in Court Road incorporates Sherard Hall and two meeting rooms and was built as the Congregational Church in 1936. The original church at the corner of Well Hall Road and the High Street was demolished to make way for Burton's, the Tailors, (now 55 High Street). The Victorian church of All Saints at Bercta Road, New Eltham was completed with a permanent chancel in 1931 together with vestries and Lady Chapel. The church of St. Thomas More and St. John Fisher was then also of unique design and stands on a site once reserved for a permanent Anglican Church of St. Barnabas. Finance came from a lady who lived at Crowborough, Sussex, and the foundation stone was laid in 1936 with the church being dedicated in the following year. Our Lady Help of Christians Church in Mottingham Road celebrated its first mass in 1933 and the cost of the new church was almost defrayed by two wins on the Irish Sweeps horse race.

For the new housing districts shopping parades were constructed which were let to various traders who provided the necessities for basic living as grocers, newsagents and tobacconists, off licences, butchers, greengrocers, chemists, hardware store, etc. Almost every new parade seemed incomplete without a branch of the R.A.C.S. (Royal Arsenal Co-operative Society) which could incorporate grocery and butchery facilities with the attraction of the "tin checks," a form of dividend which was claimed annually.

The Westhorne Avenue Branch of the R.A.C.S., c. 1929

J.K.C.

Larger outlets of neighbourhood shops were to be found in the High Street, with specialist shops providing for other needs like clothing and household goods. Many additions were made to the range of shops which included Hind's department store (1934), 145 High Street, and directly opposite was the Royal Arsenal Co-operative Society Food and Economy Stores basement shop (1935) at 168 High Street. This was the Co-op's answer to the attractions of Woolworth's (1933) at 173 High Street. The Arcade (1930) created small shop units in a different form to anything seen before in Eltham. Due to the financial difficulties of the original developers the planned 31 shops were not constructed even though houses in Messeter Place and Elm Terrace were demolished for the scheme.

Many of the newer developments followed widening of the
High Street which was commenced by Woolwich Borough Council
in the early 1920's after property and front gardens were
purchased.   The single storey shops to the east of the
National Westminster Bank (65 High Street) were known as 1-14
Merlewood Parade when completed as they stood mainly on the
site of the demolished Merlewood House.   No.4 Merlewood
Parade (73 High Street) opened in December 1923 as
Williamson's which served high class teas, refreshments and
confectionery.   Surviving for several years after World War
II, it was a popular refreshment stop.

The single storey shops which were originally
known as Merlewood Parade, 1990   *S.F.C.*

The Hind's store was built as a two storey building which
only went as far as the present staircase. Extensions in 1936
brought extra floors, lift and a roof garden where teas were
provided. Further extensions were possible in the late 1950's
after the Jubilee Cottages were demolished to the rear of the
store. The name was changed to Allder's in 1978.

Woolwich Borough Council had been producing its own electricity since the turn of the century and on council owned land next to Eltham Library a new electricity showroom was erected in the early 1930's which incorporated an upstairs office for the local Registrar of births, marriages and deaths. The long-awaited swimming baths were opened at Eltham Hill on 4th April 1939 but the early euphoria of carefree swimming sessions was dimmed as the storm clouds of World War II were appearing on the horizon. Unknowingly, Eltham and its residents were to be subjected to six years of uncertainty and sacrifice.

Firemen at King's Park School preparing for the next chapter in Eltham's history   *J.K.C.*

ELTHAM c. 1936

MONETARY EQUIVALENTS TABLE

The United Kingdom changed its monetary system from £ s d to decimal in 1971. For the benefit of those unfamiliar with the old monetary system a table of equivalent values is shown below.

£	s	d		£	p	(approximate value)
		0.25	(Farthing)		0.1	
		0.5	(Halfpenny)		0.2	
		0.75	(Three farthings)		0.3	
		1			0.5	
		3			1.25	
		6	(Tanner)		2.5	
	1	0	(Bob)		5	
	2	0	(Florin)		10	
	2	6	(Half Crown)		12.5	
	5	0	(Crown)		25	
	10	0			50	
1	0	0		1 .	00	
1	1	0	(21s = 1 Guinea)	1 .	5	

NOTE

d = penny (old penny)
s = shilling
12d = 1s
20s = £1
20s = 240d = £1

LIST OF SUBSCRIBERS Cont...

.G. & V. Page, Minehead, Somerset

'id Parker, Eltham

.J. Parsons, Canterbury, Kent

ncis C. Pentelow, Eltham

E.J.E. Percival & Mrs. M.E. Percival, Sidcup

dys Perkins & In Mem., Cissie Langton, Eltham

n W. & Grace Perry, Eltham

lrey Jeanne Pert, Mottingham

& Mariette Pilbeam, New Eltham

& Don Piper, Mottingham

s Elaine Pitcher & Mr. Darren McNaughton, Mottingham

ert A. & Dilys M. Pittman, Mottingham

mond Pope, D.L., Sidcup

n Priestley, Edinburgh

cent C. Randall, Eltham

. A.M. Read, New Eltham

is Reynolds, Wittersham, Kent

& Arthur Robinson, South Darenth, Kent

M. & Elizabeth Russell, Eltham

& Colin Rutt, Eltham

& M.L. Sangster, New Eltham

& Diana P. Sargeant, Sidcup

d Shepherd, Wittersham, Kent

ert & Hazel Simmons, Eltham

rk Simmons, New Eltham

Roger & Sally Simmons, New Eltham

Francis E. Skilleter & Peter G. Patrick, Eltham

Bernard & Gwen Skinner, Eltham

D.J. Skinner, Eltham

Geoff & Angela Smith, Eltham

Mr. & Mrs. P. Smith, Eltham

Charlotte & Rachel Smith, Eltham

Peter Dudley Smith & Beryl Smith, New Eltham

Phyllis & Hayden Smith, Eltham

Mrs. K.M. Spooner, Eltham

Miss Eileen Hext Stonham, Eltham

Miss L.J. Sullivan, Mr. & Mrs. G.A. Sullivan, Eltham

Mr. & Mrs. R.G. Sullivan & Mark Sullivan, Eltham

Mr. & Mrs. S.J.M. Sullivan & Benjamin Sullivan, Eltham

Mrs. Irene Swanton, Mottingham

Mrs. M. LePage, Wanneroo, Australia

Jill Talley, Eltham

Evelyn & Margaret Taylor, New Eltham

William F. Temple (In Mem.), Folkestone, Kent

C.W.M & J.C. Thomas, New Eltham

Mrs. E. Marjorie Thorp, Eltham

Mrs. Barbara Thorpe, Eltham

Mrs. I.F. Thorpe & Mrs. G.I. Gillman, Eltham

Will & Elsie Tjaden, Welling

Miss Audrey Towell, New Eltham

LIST OF SUBSCRIBERS Cont...

Mr. J. Towey, Eltham

A.J. Turnham, Sidcup

Eileen & Bill Walsh, Eltham

Miss Joyce Walter, Eltham

John G. & Jean Wells, Eltham

G. Gordon West, Crowborough, Sussex

Colin White, Eltham

Eric J. White, Haywards Heath, Sussex

Bernard & Deirdre Williams, Eltham

Gladys M. & E.F. Wilson, New Eltham

Ross & Penny Woollard, Grove Park

John & Mary Wootton, Eltham

George & Jo Worrall, Eltham

Mr. A.M. Wotton, New Eltham

Doris & Stan Wright, Eltham

Mrs. Frances A. Yorath, Eltham

The Loyal George Chester Lodge of the Independent Order of
Odd Fellows Manchester Unity Friendly Society

SOME ELTHAM PERSONALITIES

Thomas Doggett (1650-1721) is remembered as the instigator of the annual River Thames boat race which bears his name with the winner receiving a distinctive scarlet coat and metal badge. Originating in 1715 it is the oldest sporting event in the world and was started by Doggett to commemorate "the glorious accession to the English throne of George 1". He was born in Dublin and had acting associations with London theatres including Drury Lane where he was the manager. He lived his last years in Eltham and was buried at St John's Church in September 1721 where a commemorative plaque can be seen on the outer south wall. His wife was the grand-daughter of an Eltham vicar.

Jeffrey Farnol (1878-1952) the novelist, lived at 71 Eltham Road c. 1911-1925 and spent some of his youth at 9 Dorville Road, Lee. He wrote historical novels starting with "The Broad Highway" in 1910; "The Amateur Gentleman"(1913) refers to The White Hart of Eltham Village in Chapter L11.

Charles Folkard (1878-1963) the illustrator, created the mouse character Teddy Tail which was the first daily newspaper strip when it appeared in the Daily Mail in 1915. He lived at 2 Balcaskie Road, Eltham and for many years at 2 Court Farm Road, Mottingham. He illustrated many children's books and some of his drawings were recently purchased by Colfe's School as a memorial to a former pupil.

George Goschen (1831-1907) spent his youth at a house now known as the St Mary's Community and Resource Centre in Eltham High Street. After his marriage he lived at Eagle House, now The Presbytery adjoining Christ Church in Eltham High Street. He became Member of Parliament for the City of London and went on to achieve high political office, including that of First Lord of The Admiralty and Chancellor of the Exchequer. In 1900 he was created Viscount Goschen of Hawkhurst. A room at St Mary's Community Centre is named after him.

SOME ELTHAM PERSONALITIES Cont...

Denis Healey was born at Mottingham on 30th August 1917 and lived at 2 Rosyth Road in one of the Eltham Hutments. When he was five years old the family moved to Yorkshire where his father took up the appointment of Principal at Keighley Technical College. He has been a Member of Parliament since 1952 and held the office of Defence Secretary and Chancellor of the Exchequer.

Bob Hope was born at 44 Craigton Road, Eltham on 29th May 1903 and named Leslie Townes Hope. His father was a stonemason and his grandfather was a partner in the firm of Picton and Hope who built the houses in Craigton Road for developer Mr A. Cameron Corbett. At the age of 18 months Bob left Eltham to live with his family in Bristol before their emigration to America in 1908. His success as a comedian and film star particularly in the 'Road' series has made him an international star. The renamed Bob Hope Theatre in Wythfield Road, Eltham has been helped financially by a British Golf Tournament associated with Bob Hope. He visited Eltham in 1980 and 1982.

Frankie Howerd (1922-   ) was born in York and came to Eltham when he was 2½ years old. The family lived in one of the Eltham Hutments at 19a Arbroath Road and Frankie attended activities connected with St Barnabas Church which was then at the end of his road. He attended Shooters Hill Grammar School. Since the War his comedy talents have been featured on radio, T.V. and in films and he has been the recipient of the O.B.E. He returned to Eltham in October 1988 to open the renewed St Barnabas Church Hall which has been renamed "The Frankie Howerd Centre".

Rex Whistler (1905-1944) was born at 5 Park Place (now Passey Place) on 24th June 1905. His father was a local builder trading as 'Whistler and Worge' and in 1907 the family moved to "Bryher" in Court Road (now site of the United Reform Church). Rex showed early talent as an artist and later trained at the Slade School of Art. As well as book illustrations and designs for theatre productions he produced detailed wall paintings for wealthy patrons. An early work is at the restaurant in the Tate Gallery and later commissions include the Tent Room at Port Lympne, Hythe, Kent and at the Dining Room at Plas Newydd on the Isle of Anglesey. He was killed in action at Normandy in the Second World War.

ABOUT THE AUTHORS

Clifford Crate

Clifford Crate has been an Eltham resident since 1921 when he was brought from his Plumstead birthplace to a family home on the developing Page Estate at the age of 4. He was educated at the Eltham National School, Roper Street and the Eltham Central School, Deansfield Road. His first job was in the City. In 1940 he was called to serve in the Royal Navy and became Leading Cook on corvettes in the Atlantic and Indian Oceans. On demobilisation he returned to Siemens Bros, finally becoming manager of a large department. Through all these years Clifford Crate has always been interested in watching Eltham change from village to suburb. He saw Westhorne Avenue being built and watched the first tram run along this new road. He retired in 1982, took on an allotment, became a member of the Eltham Society, and has been its Chairman since October 1987. He is also active in other local charities.

John Kennett

John Kennett has lived in Eltham for most of his life and teaches in Plumstead. While working at Eltham C. of E. School he conceived the idea of starting an Eltham Society and became its first Secretary in November 1965. Since then he has held several positions including Chairman of the Society and is currently Chairman of the Amenity Committee. His keen interest in the history of Eltham has been used in his "Eltham Past and Present " adult education class. He is a regular contributor to the Eltham Society's Newsletter and has given many public lectures on various aspects of Eltham's history.

Sally Simmons

Sally Simmons has lived all her life in Eltham and for as long as she can remember has been interested in the history of the district. A State Registered Medical Laboratory Scientist, she is now a housewife, who has recently obtained a Diploma (with Distinction) in Local History at the University of London. She was the Secretary of the Eltham Society from 1972-1988 and still serves on its Council and Local History Committee. She is also a member of the London Wildlife Trust and serves as a member of its LESSA Pond Committee.

ABOUT THE AUTHORS Cont...

Lesley Sullivan

From the age of one Lesley Sullivan has lived on the Corbett Estate in Eltham. Her interest in history began whilst attending Prendergast School at Catford, where she obtained her History "A" Level. She currently works for an insurance company in London. In her spare time she has attended local history classes, is a member of the Eltham Society Local History Committee and helps to run the Boys Brigade at a local church.

Margaret Taylor

Margaret Taylor became interested in history during her primary school years. She gained a distinction in the subject at the end of her own training for a teaching career and gained a Diploma in History with Merit, from London University, in 1971. She has lived in New Eltham all her life and is currently Deputy Head of Horn Park Junior School, Lee. During what are laughingly called her "leisure" hours she has been an active member of the Eltham Society since its foundation, and was its Chairman from 1980-1987. She shared in the writing of other Eltham Society publications from 1970 and also wrote the guidebooks for Eltham Church (St. John's) in 1975 and 1985. She has acted as Honorary Archivist for that church since 1966. She served as its Churchwarden from 1974-1980 and from 1982 has been one of the Trustees of the Leggatt's Charity founded in Eltham in 1714.

Roger Simmons

Roger Simmons has lived in Eltham since early childhood. He has been interested in local history and amenity matters for many years. From 1971-1974 he represented New Eltham ward as a councillor for the London Borough of Greenwich. A member of the Eltham Society since 1970 he has served on its Amenity Committee and was Vice-Chairman of the Society for some years. Roger is a technical author by profession, being a Fellow of the Institute of Scientific and Technical Communicators, and is currently Chairman of the Publications Committee.

SOURCES AND BIBLIOGRAPHY

A list of principal sources and their whereabouts to aid future research into the history of Eltham.

Primary Printed Sources.

1   Anglo-Saxon Chronicle.

2   Domesday Book, Phillimore edition for Kent, 1983.

Primary Manuscript Sources.

3   Documents relating to the manor of Eltham in the Archives of Westminster Abbey.

4   Documents relating to the manor of Eltham in the Public Record Office.

5   Parish records of Eltham.
             Churchwardens' Accounts from 1554.
             Registers from 1583.

6   Wills and Inventories   relating   to Eltham residents in Kent Record Office, Maidstone.

7   Tithe Map and Apportionment of Eltham, 1840.

8   Census Returns, 1841, in Public Record Office.

9   Census Returns, 1851, in Public Record Office.

SOURCES AND BIBLIOGRAPHY Cont...

Secondary Printed Sources.

10   Archaeological reports on the locality to be
            found in the local history collections of the
            London Boroughs of Bexley, Bromley and
            Greenwich.

11   Articles on Anglo-Saxon charters to be found in
            the local history collections of the London
            Boroughs of Bexley and Bromley.

12   K.P. Witney, THE JUTISH FOREST, Athlone Press,
            1976.

13   R. Rigden, THE ROMANS IN GREENWICH, London
            Borough of Greenwich, 1974.

14   Christopher Taylor, VILLAGE AND FARMSTEAD,
            George Philip, 1983.

15   S. Simmons & M. Taylor, HOW OLD IS THE OLD
            HOME? Unpublished essay deposited in
            Greenwich Local History Collection, 1986.

16   E.J.Priestley, THE MANOR AND PALACE OF ELTHAM,
            KENT 1086-1663. Thesis deposited in University
            of London Library.

17   R.R.C. Gregory, THE STORY OF ROYAL ELTHAM,
            1909.

18   R. Brook, THE STORY OF ELTHAM PALACE, Harrap,
            1960.

19   R. Rigden, A TUDOR BUILDING AT WELL HALL, London
            Borough of Greenwich, 1970.

SOURCES AND BIBLIOGRAPHY Cont...

20   Margaret Evans, "ELTHAM LODGE AND THE SHAW FAMILY," 1986.
        Unpublished thesis deposited at Greenwich Local History Library.

21   Margaret Evans, "LIFE IN 18TH CENTURY ELTHAM," 1985.
        Unpublished thesis deposited at Greenwich Local History Library.

22   Joyce Marlow, THE UNCROWNED QUEEN OF IRELAND, THE LIFE OF KITTY O'SHEA, Weidenfeld and Nicolson, 1975.

23   R. Kidner, THE DARTFORD LOOP LINE, Oakwood Press, 1966

24   E. Course, THE BEXLEYHEATH RAILWAY, Oakwood Press, 1980

25   D. Shorney, A HISTORY OF AVERY HILL COLLEGE, 1989.

26   Rev. Rowsell, THE ELTHAM GOLF CLUB HOUSE, 1894.

27   I. Henderson & D. Stirk, ROYAL BLACKHEATH GOLF CLUB, 1981.

28   Dictionary of National Biography for details of the lives of Richard Jefferies and E.V. Lucas.

29   Various histories of churches that have been deposited in the Greenwich Local History Library.

SOURCES AND BIBLIOGRAPHY Cont...

30   Margaret Evans, "ELTHAM 1900-1918, A CHANGING
SOCIETY?", 1989.
Unpublished thesis deposited at Greenwich Local
History Library.

31   LOOKING INTO ELTHAM, Eltham Society, 1980.

32   J. Kennett, TRAMS IN ELTHAM, 1910-1952. 1972.

33   J. Kennett, THE ELTHAM HUTMENTS, 1984.

34   The oral reminiscences of Mrs. D.M. Adye of
Craigton Road, Eltham, who was born in a house
next to St. Johns Church, Eltham.

35   Booklet for the Official Opening of the Page
Estate, deposited in the Greenwich Local History
Library.

36   Material on the Royal Arsenal Co-operative Society,
deposited in the Greenwich Local History Library.

37   Woolwich Borough Council Minutes

38   Eltham Times

39   Kentish Independent

SOURCE REFERENCE BY CHAPTER

CHAPTER 1.   1,10,11,12,13,14,15

CHAPTER 2   2,3,4,15,16,17,18

CHAPTER 3   4,5,6,17,18,19

CHAPTER 4   4,5,6,17,18,20

CHAPTER 5   5,17,20,21

CHAPTER 6   7,8,9,17

CHAPTER 7   22,23,24,25,26,27,28,29

CHAPTER 8   17,25,30,31,32,33,34

CHAPTER 9   31,32,33,35,36,37,38,39

SUGGESTIONS FOR FURTHER READING
ABOUT ELTHAM

E.F.E.Jefferson, THE WOOLWICH STORY, 1890-1965, 1970.

W.T. Vincent, SOME RECORDS OF WOOLWICH, 1890.

E.A., ELTHAM IN PAST TIMES, 1910.

Rev. Elphinstone Rivers, SOME RECORDS OF ELTHAM, 1904.

LOOKING AT ELTHAM, Eltham Society, 1970.

M.Taylor, E. NESBIT IN ELTHAM, Eltham Society, 1974.

J. Chandley & M. Taylor, THE TARN, Eltham Society, 1987.

The Greenwich Local History Library at "Woodlands," Mycenae Road, London, S.E.3, has a large collection of material relating to Eltham and the staff welcome visitors.

SUGGESTIONS FOR GENERAL READING
ON LOCAL HISTORY

W.G. Hoskins, LOCAL HISTORY IN ENGLAND, 3rd Edition, Longmans, 1984.

J.R. Ravensdale, HISTORY ON YOUR DOORSTEP, British Broadcasting Corporation, 1982.

W.E. Tate, THE PARISH CHEST, 3rd Edition Cambridge University Press, 1969.

NATWEST FOR THE PERSONAL TOUCH IN BANKING

Come and see The Action Bank. You'll find we look after all our personal customer accounts, large or small, with the same expertise.

So remember, if you want <u>efficient</u> people working on your account call in at NatWest.

NatWest

THE ACTION BANK

INDEX

E

F

G

H

I

Independent Chapel   78
Ireland, John   26
Itinerary, Antonine   8

J

Jefferies, Richard   73
Jubilee   57,87
Jubilee Cottages   57,99

K

Keightley   28
Kent   8,9,13,14,15,
    17,29,38,43,47,49,74
Kent Water Works   69
Keynsham Abbey   15
Kidbrooke   11,26
King, Dr. David   59,60,61
Kirk's Yard   60,70

L

Lambarde, William   29,32
Lannoy Road   68
Larke, John   26
Lassa Road   79
Lathes   9
Lee   11,12,13,14,
    40,68,70,72,82
Leggatt's Charity   58
Leggatt, Elizabeth   54
Lewisham   10,14,19,
    90,92,93
Library   40,50,80,99
Lilburne   40
London   23,27,30,31,34,
    38,47,48,49,55,69,
    70,72,74,78,90
London County Council
    70,72,76,87,94,95
Loop Line   67,68,77
Lucas, E.V.   73
Lyme Farm   75,77

M

Madras Villas   63
Man of Kent (The)   73
Mandeville   16,19,20
Manor   16,19,40,49,54
Market   14,17
Martyrs   26
Mayerne   33
Meadow   7,13,41,51,62,
    75,77,88,94
Mellin's   60
Memorial Hospital   7
Memorials in church
    28,52,63
Merchland Road   68
Merlewood House/Parade
    60,98
Methodist Church   78
Metropolitan Police   72
Middle Park   18,31,38,
    62,73,77,89,90,95,96
Milestones   72
Miller, Hugh   32,35,43
Montrose House   69
More, Sir Thomas   25,26
Mottingham   7,10,11,14,
    19,62,67,77,88,93,95,96
Mottingham Lane   85,87

N

National School
    29,58,68,84
Nesbit, E.   85
New Cross Turnpike Trust
    48,55,72
New Eltham   14,28,42,
    68,69,72,77,88,96
New Ideal Homesteads   93
North Park   67,74
North, Colonel   73,76
Novar Road   68

S

Saunders, R. 59
Saxons 8,10
Schools 29,32,58,
68,78,84,90,94
Scriven Alley 70
Scudds' Omnibus 62,70
Sewers 69,88
Shaw family 40,41,42,
49,50,51,52
Shaw-Brooke,
Rev. J.K. 57,58,61
Sheep 21,43,48
Sherard Road 30,59,76,
79,92,93
Shooters Hill 7,8,11,
13,14,17,31,42,54,63,
77,78,83,88,91,95
Sidcup 71,87,88,91,93
Silver Jubilee 87
Smallwood, James 42
Soils 7,9,14,20,69,88
Soup Society 61
South Circular 88
South Eastern and
Chatham Railway 77,78
Southend 14,42,62
Southend Crescent 41,63,93
Southwood Road 63,68,96
Spanish Armada 31
Spencer Gardens 79
St. Barnabas' Church 96
St. Luke's Church 78,79
St. Mary Cray 8
St. Mary's Convent 63
Stage Coaches 47,49,72
Star (The) 47
Starbuck 31,39,67,68
Stations 62,67,76,
77,78,79,88,92,93
Statutes of Eltham 25
Stocks 37
Stoney Alley 12
Streams 7,10,11,13,17
Strongbow Road
and Crescent 31
Sulong 13
Sun Yard 60,70
Survey (1605)
11,20,33,37
Swimming Pools 80,88,99

T

Tapestries 38
Textus Roffensis 15
Thames 9,14,90
Theobalds Cottages 63
Thorpe, John 23
Tillings, Thomas 70,76
Tithe Plan 62
Tobacco 42
Tollgates 49,72
Traffic Lights 91
Trams 81,85,92
Tucker, T.T. 85
Tudor Barn 25,48
Turnpike 48,55,72

U

Unemployment
33,39,52,87,88

V

Van Dyke, Sir Anthony 33
Victoria Road 67
Victoria, Queen 74,75

W

War Memorial   83
Watling Street   8,11,17
Well Hall   14,17,22,
    25,26,31,34,48,62,76,
        77,81,85,92,93,96
Well Hall Garden City   83
Well Hall House   48,85
Well Hall Road
    12,48,79,81,83,91,96
Welling   7,92,93
West End Green   30,34
West Park   67
West Kent Sewer   69
Westhorne Avenue   81,88,92
Westmount Road   91
Whipping Post   37
White Hart (The)   37,60
White Swan (The)   47
Wiklond   19,20
William I   13
Windmills   31,35
Wolsey, Cardinal   25
Wonersh Lodge   74
Wood, Benjamin   74
Woodland   7,9,13,14,
    19,20,33,39,62,77,88
Woolwich   7,10,12,14,
    19,30,39,61,62,76,
        81,83,90,92,94,96
Woolwich Borough
        Council   74,80,
    85,88,89,95,98,99
Woolwich, Mayor of   88,94
Workhouse   47,52,53,55
World War I   83
Wricklemarsh   14
Wyatt's Elm   28
Wyborne   32,36,68,94
Wyncham Stream   7,13
Wythens, William   42

The Eltham Society would like to thank the management and staff of Solitaire Ltd., Greenwich, London S.E.10 for their help and advice in making the printing of this publication possible.